FASHION TRENDS

Understanding Fashion Series

ISSN 1753-3406

Understanding Fashion is a series of short, accessible, authored books designed to provide students with a map of the fashion field. The books are aimed at beginning undergraduate students and they are designed to cover an entire module. Accessibly written, each book will include boxed case studies, bullet point chapter summaries, guides to further reading, and questions for classroom discussion. Individual titles can be used as a key text or to support a general introductory survey. They will be of interest to students studying fashion from either an applied or cultural perspective.

Titles in the series will include:

Fashion Design
Elizabeth Bye

Fashion and the Consumer
Jennifer Yurchisin and Kim K.P. Johnson

Fashion and Identity
Alison Goodrum

Understanding Fashion and Textiles
Jess Power

Fashion Trends: Analysis and Forecasting
Eundeok Kim, Ann Marie Fiore and Hyejeong Kim

FASHION TRENDS
Analysis and Forecasting

Eundeok Kim, Ann Marie Fiore and Hyejeong Kim

BLOOMSBURY

LONDON • NEW DELHI • NEW YORK • SYDNEY

Bloomsbury Academic
An imprint of Bloomsbury Publishing Plc

50 Bedford Square   175 Fifth Avenue
London   New York
WC1B 3DP   NY 10010
UK   USA

www.bloomsbury.com

English edition first published in 2011 by Berg
Reprinted by Bloomsbury Academic 2013

© Eundeok Kim, Ann Marie Fiore and Hyejeong Kim, 2011

Eundeok Kim, Ann Marie Fiore and Hyejeong Kim have asserted
their right under the Copyright, Designs and Patents Act, 1988,
to be identified as Author of this work.

No responsibility for loss caused to any individual or organization
acting on or refraining from action as a result of the material in
this publication can be accepted by Bloomsbury or the author.

British Library Cataloguing-in-Publication Data
A catalogue record for this book is available from the British Library.

ISBN: HB: 978-1-8478-8294-3
PB: 978-1-8478-8293-6

Library of Congress Cataloging-in-Publication Data
A catalog record for this book is available from the Library of Congress.

Typeset by Apex CoVantage, LLC
Printed and bound in Great Britain

CONTENTS

ILLUSTRATIONS

ACKNOWLEDGEMENTS

Many individuals have contributed directly and indirectly to the creation of this book, and the authors are grateful to all of them. In particular, we thank Kim Johnson and Alison Goodrum, coeditors of the book series *Understanding Fashion*, for the idea for this unique book series and for their support and valuable comments. We also appreciate the staff at Berg who contributed to the project, including Anna Wright and Julia Hall, for their tireless assistance.

We would also like to express our gratitude to many of our colleagues in academia and in the textile and apparel industry who shared their expertise and insight. Particularly, we thank Billie Collier at Florida State University for providing relevant literature, Chungmin Lee at PFIN for interviewing and offering images of visual materials, Jean McElvain at the Goldstein Museum at the University of Minnesota for providing images, and Stylesight, WGSN, Color Marketing Group, and The Doneger for offering images and relevant information. Finally, heartfelt thanks to our families and friends for their endless support and understanding throughout the creation of the book.

INTRODUCTION

Fashion is continuously in motion. New styles are introduced in the market, gain popularity by being accepted by more and more consumers, reach the stages of maturity, and go out of fashion acceptance. This process, called a fashion cycle, helps forecasters and retailers anticipate the acceptance and duration of fashion trends. New fashions are innovations. Yet, fashion is considered evolutionary rather than revolutionary, which means there is a perceivable progression across styles from season to season that results in an identifiable fashion trend. *Fashion Trends: Analysis and Forecasting* describes the mechanism of a fashion trend and the impetus behind fashion change. The progression of a trend or fashion change mirrors changes in social, cultural, economical, and technological factors within a society. We will illustrate how past trends reflect subcultural influences, the art, music, architecture, and consumer lifestyle changes of a time period. Although past fashion provides designers with inspiration, these fashions are updated to meet the sensibilities of today's consumer.

Fashion change is not a simple process. Not only is it affected by a complex interplay among sociocultural factors, such as concerns for sustainability and declining economic conditions, but also it is affected by features of the product experience (e.g., how easily one can see others adopting the trend) and of consumers (e.g., their tendency to quickly adopt new trends). Additionally, fashion change can originate in a particular social group, trickling up from the streets or trickling down from top designers, or move across all social groups simultaneously. Adding another layer of complexity, fashion is a global phenomenon not limited to developed countries such as Japan, the United Kingdom, and the United States. Global consumers inspire fashion innovations and share new fashion trends through the Internet and other media, which accelerates fashion change across time and space. By maintaining efficiency and flexibility throughout production and distribution systems and by utilizing information and communication technologies, fashion companies are capable of producing and selling their merchandise in various locations across the globe and responding quickly to changing fashion trends. This phenomenon is called "fast fashion" and is offered by such companies as Zara and H&M. Fast-changing fashion has made understanding fashion trends even more complex than before.

Having a grasp of future trends and their longevity is an important currency for companies, enabling them to develop products and marketing strategies that fit their target customers' needs and preferences. This is the role of forecasting. Forecasting is a creative and analytical process, involving not only the observation of changes in fashion but also the analysis and synthesis of information from an array of sources inside and outside the fashion business. It involves extensive data collection related to consumers and past sales, using quantitative and qualitative techniques. Many fashion firms use forecasting companies to provide insight into upcoming trends. Forecasting companies observe emerging trends that originate around the world and gather information through interviews with major visionaries in design, art, music, architecture, culture, politics, technology, and marketing. Forecasting firms also look at subcultural influences, consumer lifestyles and preferences, and demographics. Integration and analysis of information from these various sources allow forecasting companies to predict future direction for fashion.

Forecasting color, fabric, and silhouette directions is both a fun and a serious undertaking because these forecasts affect a fashion business's long- and short-term decisions. Executives use forecasts to establish their long-term vision or to direction for an organization. Managers use forecasts to establish the marketing strategies they will use to effectively position their products. Designers, merchandisers, and buyers utilize the forecasts of trends in color, fabric, and silhouette to develop or buy merchandise for upcoming seasons.

Fashion Trends: Analysis and Forecasting is designed to help students understand how trend forecasts are created and employed by various professionals in the fashion industry to improve a firm's competitiveness in the marketplace. This text is intended for students enrolled in fashion trend and forecasting classes in their first or second year of postsecondary study. Why is it important to study the fashion trend and forecasting process? The fashion industry is one of the largest employment sectors in the world and includes manufacturing, marketing, and retailing sectors. Professionals in these sectors work together and are united in their dependence on trend analysis and forecasting. For instance, yarn and textile manufacturers, designers, and merchandisers use forecasts to develop merchandise for the upcoming season. Thus, to effectively communicate with other professionals in the fashion industry and to be successful in their own careers, it is essential for fashion students to fully understand the role and importance of trend forecasting and how it is and can be used by various individuals working in different fashion sectors.

Fashion Trends includes seven chapters. The first chapter discusses important terms related to fashion trends and forecasting that the student should understand. The content of this chapter addresses the major factors influencing fashion change in the twentieth century and the theories explaining the sources of fashion leadership. Chapter 2 outlines the attributes of both innovations and consumers that influence the acceptance and the rate of adoption of new fashion offerings. This chapter discusses how fashion professionals can use these attributes to accelerate fashion adoption and business success. Chapter 3 examines the process and methods of fashion trend analysis and forecasting. It includes a discussion of short- and long-term forecasts and closes with a discussion of the future of forecasting. Chapter 4 addresses the role of fashion industry professionals—developers, gatekeepers, and promoter—in creating and supporting trends. Various forecasting companies and their services are discussed in detail. Chapter 5 outlines factors that have accelerated fashion product innovation and adoption, including the presence of style-confident consumers and industry technology. This chapter also illustrates how a fashion firm can use consumer- and industry-related trends to facilitate the adoption of innovations. Chapter 6 reinforces the importance of sustainability and social responsibility in today's fashion industry. This chapter addresses the influence of social responsibility on fashion trends, such as consumer trends toward green products, consumer trends against the use of real fur or leather, and consumer trends toward recycled fashion. Finally, chapter 7 addresses forecasting presentation, including the process of sorting, organizing, and editing materials; searching for relationships and patterns; and creating the meaning to be conveyed in a presentation. This chapter introduces different formats for trend forecasts and discusses each, focusing on trend maps, trend boards, and oral presentations. Through this book, students will be able to understand the role and process of fashion forecasting and how the information can be used by various fashion professionals, from executives establishing long-term marketing strategies to designers developing merchandise for upcoming seasons.

1

THE BASICS OF FASHION TRENDS AND FORECASTING

Objectives

- Understand important terms related to fashion trends and forecasting
- Understand the fashion trends and influences in the twentieth century
- Understand the tempo of fashion change and the direction of fashion change
- Understand the concepts of fashion trend analysis and forecasting

Introduction to fashion trend terminology

One cannot look at fashion magazines, Web sites, or blogs without seeing the "trends," "key trends for the season," "fashion and color trends," or "makeup trends." The term "trend" is often used interchangeably with "fashion" when the writer is referring to fashion-forward items. The term, "fashion" is also confused with the term "style" because some writers use "fashionable" and "stylish" interchangeably. The term "style" is also confused with "design." What exactly is a trend, fashion, style, or design? What are the differences among these terms? The first step in understanding fashion trends is to define these terms.

Trend, style, design, and fashion

A **trend** refers to a general direction or movement (Stone, 2008). For example, if you see in fashion magazines that "there is a trend toward faux furs," it means that upscale designers have shown faux fur coats or details on the runway, apparel retailers have started to introduce them in their catalogs or stores, and some fashion-forward consumers are wearing faux fur items.

Designers usually start conceptualizing products for a new season one year prior to the actual selling season. Therefore, for apparel retailers, knowing what customers will want to wear next season is much more than just helpful information—it is requisite for success. When apparel retailers recognize fashion trends and develop their merchandise on the basis of that information, they increase the probability that consumers will accept merchandise when it arrives in stores. Trends are not limited to apparel, accessories, and cosmetics; they can be found in various other consumer products, including home décor, furniture, automobiles, and electronics. Therefore, a trend toward purple is important information not only for apparel retailers but also for the cosmetics and electronics (e.g., computers) industries. Designers and other professionals in the fashion and creative industries access trend information through trend forecasting companies, which are discussed in detail in chapter 4.

A **style**, broadly speaking, is "a characteristic mode of presentation that typifies several similar objects of the same category or class" (Sproles & Burns, 1994, p. 7). Styles exist not only in apparel but also in architecture, painting, music, and politics. We often speak of "punk," "hippie," "Empire," or "Baroque" styles. Some celebrities, such as Lady Gaga, Madonna, and Elvis Presley, have created their own distinctive styles. Although we recognize these styles, it does not necessarily mean that the styles are adopted by a large group of people. We can identify the Lady Gaga style, but how many of us have actually tried it? When the term is used in apparel, a style refers to distinctive characteristics within a specific category (Sproles & Burns, 1994). For instance, in the skirt category, there are several styles, including miniskirts, pencil skirts, A-line skirts, and pleated skirts.

Design is "a unique combination of silhouette, construction, fabric, and details that distinguishes a single fashion object from all other objects of the same category or classes" (Sproles & Burns 1994, p. 6). Within each style, there can be numerous designs, but they share common design components, which distinguish the style from other styles. For example, the hippie style shares design components, such as fringed hems, bell-bottom silhouettes, tie-dyed surfaces, and embroidery. A hoodie is a style, and Juicy Couture offers various hoodie designs, differentiated through various embroidery patterns, fabrics (e.g., velour or French terry), or trims (e.g., chain or ruffle).

While a style may not be widely accepted by people, a **fashion** is "a style of consumer product or way of behaving that is temporarily adopted by a discernible proportion of members of a social group because that chosen style or behavior is perceived to be socially appropriate for the time and situation" (Sproles & Burns 1994, p. 4). Of course, the term "fashion" is often associated with apparel, but there can be fashions in other consumer product categories, as well as in ideas and behaviors. Examples of fashions in hairstyles include Jennifer Aniston's "Rachel" cut, which more than eleven million women have tried, and Victoria Beckham's short, asymmetrical bob, another favorite hairstyle with women in every age group ("Ten most popular. . . ," 2010). An example of fashion in behavior is the use of Facebook, communication through an electronic social networking site. Since it was launched, in 2004, Facebook has rapidly spread among college students and is used all around the world. Having a Facebook account is widely accepted, and visiting sites is an everyday ritual for many people, young and old.

Fashions are temporal by nature—no fashion is everlasting! Boot-cut jeans were popular and prevalent during the early 2000s, but skinny jeans emerged as a new fashion in the mid-2000s. Some styles may become popular because they are considered to be appropriate in particular social situations. Pantsuits are popular because they are suitable for job interviews. Some styles may be accepted as a result of social pressure; people are influenced by each other and often adopt certain styles to meet the expectations of a person or group or to show their group membership or conformity (Solomon & Rabolt, 2009). Think about how many times you bought a new apparel style to fit into a group.

Fashions can be categorized based on the group to which they appeal. **High fashion** consists of a new style accepted by a limited number of innovators or leaders who want to be the first to adopt new products. High-fashion styles tend to be available in small quantities and sold at relatively high prices. Unlike high fashion, **mass fashion**, or **volume fashion**, refers to styles that are widely accepted by a large group of fashion-conscious consumers and that are produced and sold in large quantities at moderate to low prices. Mass fashion accounts for the majority of sales in the fashion business (Stone, 2008).

Fashion, fad, and classic styles

As shown in Figure 1.1, styles vary in terms of their rates of acceptance and duration. This means that styles have different life cycles. A **fashion** style is accepted and diffused among people at a moderate rate; it is slowly accepted in the beginning, rapidly rises, reach its peak, and gradually declines. A fashion style remains popular for quite a long time, having widespread acceptance among consumers. For instance,

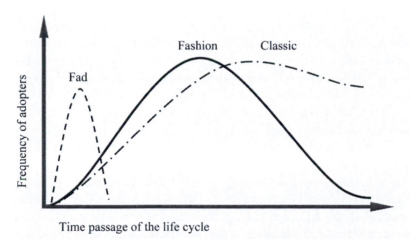

Figure 1.1   Fad, fashion, and classic styles have different rates and durations of acceptance.

Source: Adapted from Brannon, E. L. (2010). *Fashion forecasting* (3rd ed.). New York: Fairchild Books, p. 7.

wide-shouldered jackets emerged in the mid-1980s and were popular until the mid-1990s. This style then declined, with shoulder pads became gradually smaller.

A **fad** is a short-lived style. Unlike a fashion style, it becomes popular very rapidly, reaching its peak quickly, and then suddenly dies out. It tends to obtain limited rather than substantial adoption and may be accepted only in certain social and subcultural groups (Sproles & Burns, 1994). As an example, miniskirts with leggings and wide belts were popular in the mid-2000s for a short period of time among younger consumers. A fad may be revolutionary or extreme in design compared to other existing styles (Sproles & Burns, 1994). Crocs, originally developed as a spa shoe, became a fad because of its unique, comfortable design, and kiosks selling the merchandise appeared in most major shopping malls. However, the popularity did not last very long. You may also recognize past fads, such as cornrows, zoot suits, poodle skirts, wide bell-bottom pants, platform shoes, Nehru jackets, tie-dye t-shirts, leisure suits, jelly shoes, Mohawk haircuts, and beanies.

Classic styles may be adopted at a slow rate in the beginning, but the telltale sign of a classic is its staying power. Classics are widely accepted and stay in fashion for an extended period of time, with some slight variation in detail. Examples are Levi's "501" jeans, trench coats, button-down shirts, polo shirts, Chanel suits, turtleneck sweaters, blazers, pearl necklaces, and penny loafers. Think about the trench coat—it has been in fashion for years, undergoing slight variations such as changes in the size of shoulder pads or lengths, but, even with these changes, it is easily discernable as a trench coat. These styles are often basic and simple in design and, therefore, are likely to be accepted by various social groups.

Fashion trends in context

New fashions have been continuously created throughout history. Although new fashions are considered to be innovations, most of them are not greatly different from existing fashions and are modifications of previous ones (i.e., **continuous innovations**). Therefore, many new fashions tend to be evolutionary rather than revolutionary (Sproles & Burns, 1994). For example, skinny jeans were introduced in the mid-2000s and became narrower throughout the late 2000s, including evolving into skin-tight denim leggings that use stretch fabrics by 2009.

Whereas most innovations have evolved from past styles, there have been some exceptions, generally led by major social or world events, such as the end of World War II. After World War II, Christian Dior's New Look typified a revolutionary change from masculine, square-cut wartime suits for women to billowy-skirted, hourglass-shaped dresses. This radical change reflected the desire to return to tradition roles for men and women. Women were no longer needed in factories because men were back from the war to fill the positions. In addition, the fuller cut of the new look was possible because fabric was no longer in short supply because so much of it was used in the war effort.

Along with the impact of world events, fashion trends have been influenced by social (e.g., women's rights movement), subcultural influences (e.g., "Black Is Beautiful"), and economic conditions (e.g., the Depression of the 1930s). Technological advances, such as the invention of the zipper and synthetic fibers, and entertainment, such as movies and TV shows, have also influenced fashion change. In addition, fashion leaders, including designers and celebrity icons, help propel fashion change and consumers' fashion adoption. World events and social, cultural, economic, and technological changes influence one another and consequent styles. To illustrate the multiple influences on fashion, the following section discusses some of the important fashion trends between 1900 and 2010 and the events that likely influenced them.

World events

Major world events that have influenced fashion change include World War I, World War II, and the September 11, 2001, attacks on the World Trade Center and the Pentagon. World War I resulted in considerable changes in women's roles and fashion. As increasing numbers of men participated in the war, women's presence in the labor force continued to increase. They were allowed to enter many jobs for the first time in history and, ultimately, gained economic independence. As a result, significant changes occurred in women's wear, and designers focused on easy-to-wear clothing (e.g., a pull-over style blouse without fastenings worn with a skirt) that was both fashionable and practical. A designer that exemplifies easy-to-wear clothing was Gabrielle Chanel. Chanel had her first haute-couture collection in 1916, introducing simple but sensational two-piece jersey outfits that were loved by many women. In addition, designers introduced military-inspired fashions, such as tailored jackets and suits with a loose waist and patch pocket details. The color khaki was in fashion because it was the color of military uniforms (Mendes & de la Haye, 1999).

During World War II, women again worked in factories, replacing men who joined the military services, and wanted minimalist pieces that could create maximum versatility. With the declaration of war, designers in Paris and London immediately introduced styles emphasizing practicality, such as coats with hoods, suits with large slouch pockets, and bags large enough to carry a gas mask and footwear. Because of the shortage of fabric, the quantity of fabric used for garments and the number of pockets and buttons were restricted. Fabric manufacturing was controlled in support of the war effort; the availability of fabrics such as wool, silk, nylon, and rubber was limited for regular consumers (Mendes & de la Haye, 1999).

The September 11, 2001, terrorist attack in New York City and outside Washington, D.C., is considered a major world event of the new millennium, and it has had an impact on fashion trends. People expressed their feelings of patriotism, grief, and pride through fashion; items designed using the American flag, such as t-shirts, pins, and other accessories, were widely available. Consumers tended to avoid trendy, expensive items, and consumer confidence sharply dropped as people felt depressed and feared further attacks. As a result, apparel sales, particularly in the luxury market, dropped significantly, and major department and designer stores had to cancel their deliveries and reorders ("Terrorism's trauma . . . ," 2001).

Economic conditions

Under pessimistic economic conditions, consumers tend to curb their consumption, especially of luxury goods. For instance, starting in 1929, the collapse of the New York stock market led to a worldwide, economic depression and mass unemployment that lasted until the late 1930s or early 1940s. The event influenced not only the U.S. fashion industry but also the French high-fashion industry, which had been dependent on exports to U.S. retailers. U.S. department stores canceled their orders, and designers cut their prices and introduced inexpensive ready-to-wear lines (Mendes & de la Haye, 1999). The recession that began in 2008 has had a similar impact on U.S. consumers, who turned to inexpensive (store) brands, discount retailers, and basic styles for their apparel needs (Blume, 2008).

Subcultural influences

Subcultural influences are typified by unique styles that many times diffuse to the mainstream. For example, in the United States, the "Black Is Beautiful" movement began in the 1960s among African Americans who were making strides in civil rights. The movement aimed to dispel the prevailing notion, projected by the media, that black features were less attractive than white features (Anderson & Cromwell, 1977; Weedon, 2002). Thus, the movement expressed a new sense of identity among African Americans and focused on the understanding of African beauty and aesthetics (Davies, 2008). As a result of this movement, Afro hairstyles became a powerful symbol of black pride and were widely adopted by both men and women within and outside the African American community in the late 1960s.

Unemployed young people and students in the United Kingdom started punk fashion in the mid-1970s. They faced little chance of employment due to a crippling recession, and they saw government as either ineffective or corrupt (Savage, 2001). For punks, clothing and hairstyles made a statement. The punk look, which was originally a sign of antiestablishment sentiment, has since been commercialized and diffused into mass-market and high-end fashions. Popular punk styles included tight black trousers, mohair sweaters, leather jackets with paint, chains, and metal studs, Doctor Martens boots, and Mohican hairstyles (Mendes & de la Haye, 1999).

In the 1970s, African Americans and Latinos in New York originated hip-hop fashion. It became increasingly popular throughout the late 1980s and 2000s due to commercialization by major fashion companies, such as Nike, Reebok, Tommy Hilfiger, Polo Ralph Lauren, and Timberland. In addition, hip-hop fashion influenced high-fashion designers; Isaac Mizrahi and Chanel showed hip-hop-inspired fashion in their shows in the late 1980s and early 1990s, respectively (Wilbekin, 1999). In the 2000s, the influence of hip-hop fashion reached many subcultures, and specific styles, such as hoodies and sweatpants, were accepted by mainstream consumers. In addition, many hip-hop artists started their own fashion brands and clothing lines: Sean John by Diddy, Apple Bottom Jeans by Nelly, Rocawear by Jay-Z, and Shady Limited by Eminem.

Social changes

Social changes, such as changes in women's roles, including woman suffrage and increasing social participation, have created new styles and influenced fashion change. For instance, after World War I, the dominant fashion was the garçonne look, which was a boyish, youthful style, consisting of men's jackets, ties, and short hair. At that time, social, economic, and political freedom was given to a relatively small number of women. For example, in the United Kingdom, it was not until 1928 that all British women obtained suffrage; only women who were over the age of 30, married, and university graduates were entitled to vote before then. Therefore, the garçonne look, inspired by menswear, was the symbol of progressive women who pursued an independent life (Mendes & de la Haye, 1999).

The power suit, consisting of a jacket with exaggerated shoulder pads and a skirt, appeared in the 1980s as the number of working women increased. It was associated with the social improvement of women's roles and was worn to display women's status in the workplace. According to the online exhibition by the International Museum of Women ("The Power Suit," n.d.),

> The power suit connotes authority, strength, and leadership. Yet the term also implies that power—especially for women—is not a birthright as it is for men. It is something that can be acquired and put on. And something that can be stripped away. The power suit is akin to armor, outfitting a woman to do battle in a predominantly male world.

Entertainment

The styles worn by actors and actresses have an impact on fashion trends. In the 1950s, young movie stars, such as James Dean and Marlon Brando, led fashion trends. Jeans became a symbol of youth when James Dean wore them in the movie *Rebel without a Cause* (1955), and Marlon Brando popularized the black leather jacket worn in the movie *The Wild One* (1953). In the 1970s, Ralph Lauren started the menswear company Polo Fashion, inspired by classic, traditional British styling. In 1971, he introduced his first women's collection, showing men's shirts modified for women. The movies *The Great Gatsby* (1974) and *Annie Hall* (1977) played important roles in popularizing his apparel. Later, in 1983, the film *Flashdance* propelled a new trend in fashion inspired by physical fitness. Aerobic dancewear and torn sweats like those worn by the actress Jennifer Beals in the film had a strong influence on fashion. As a result, warm-up suits and athletic shoes, once reserved for sport activities, were worn as street wear. Athletic shoes replaced traditional casual shoes, and shoe stores began to carry more athletic shoe styles than traditional styles. Italian fashion designer Giorgio Armani became popular in the international market thanks to the movies *American Gigolo* (1980) and *The Untouchables* (1987).

Technological inventions, such as textile innovations and production technology, have had a great influence on fashion change. The invention of rayon, which mimics the touch and appearance of natural silk, was one of the most important textile breakthroughs in the 1920s. At first, its use was limited to linings and lingerie, but, later, rayon was employed in large quantities in the production of stockings. Although rayon stockings had an advantage in terms of price, they were less desirable than silk because they ran easily and had an unattractive shine. These drawbacks were reduced by 1926, and rayon began to be used for both daywear and eveningwear (Mendes & de la Haye, 1999).

In 1938, DuPont developed nylon. Initially, the major contribution of this fiber was in the field of hosiery because it looked like silk but was more durable. Nylon stockings were introduced to the United States in 1940 and were widely available in the market by the 1950s; during World War II, nylon was used as a parachute material (Mendes & de la Haye, 1999).

In the 1990s, technological developments, including computer-aided design (CAD) and computer-aided manufacturing (CAM), were major facilitators of mass production (Mendes & de la Haye, 1999). The Quick Response (QR) system based on these technologies has allowed fast-fashion companies such as H&M, Zara, and Forever 21 to expand their businesses internationally, providing consumers with the latest fashions at low prices.

Fashion leaders, including fashion designers and celebrities, have influenced the creation and diffusion of new styles. For instance, Gabrielle Chanel was probably the most influential designer of the twentieth century; her innovative styles affected fashion change throughout decades. She was the first designer to bring menswear items, such as trousers, into the fashionable woman's wardrobe. She also introduced costume jewelry to fashion in the 1920s. At that time, fake gems were used only to provide deceptive copies of expensive originals. Chanel broke this convention by designing jewelry with paste stones and fake pearls and wearing them herself during the day (at that time, wearing jewelry was considered appropriate only in the evening) (Mendes & de la Haye, 1999). Also, she created her signature look, the Chanel suit, in 1920, using jersey, which had been mainly used for men's sportswear. Chanel made this inexpensive, ordinary textile acceptable for top fashion. Besides Chanel, numerous designers have created new fashions and led fashion trends in the twentieth century (Table 1.1).

A number of fashion leaders have influenced mainstream fashion. John F. Kennedy was elected president of the United States in 1960, and his wife, Jacqueline Kennedy, immediately became an important fashion leader thanks to her polished style. For three years, Kennedy was on the list of America's best-dressed women. Her style in apparel was coined the "Jackie Look." It included A-line dresses, pillbox hats, chunky sunglasses, and low-heeled court shoes, and these were widely copied for the mass market.

The marriage of Diana Spencer and Prince Charles, in 1981, was a major news event of the decade. Princess Diana's wedding dress was extensively copied by the bridal industry all over the world. She became a leader of world fashion in apparel, accessories, makeup, and hairstyle. Her taste in apparel, coined the "Lady Di" look (Mendes & de la Haye, 1999, p. 231), appealed to a mass audience. For the next sixteen years, Diana had an enormous influence on mainstream fashion worldwide (Mendes & de la Haye, 1999).

Table 1.1 Designers and Their Innovative Styles in the Twentieth Century

André Courrèges	Avant-garde, young, aesthetic, futuristic, and minimalistic styles
Calvin Klein	Designer jeans, sportswear
Christian Dior	"The New Look"
Cristóbal Balenciaga	Refined, tailored styles with the innovative use of fabrics, cut, and construction
Donna Karan	City-inspired modern styles
Emanuel Ungaro	Elegant styles using organic patterns and loud color combinations
Gabrielle Chanel	Chanel suit, costume jewelry
Hubert de Givenchy	Professional designs for Audrey Hepburn and Jacqueline Kennedy
Issey Miyake	Ultra-light, washable, noncrease polyester "Pleats Please" styles
Gianni Versace	"Versace style" using striking colors, materials, and cuts
Giorgia Armani	Clean and tailored suits
Pierre Cardin	Avant-garde styles using geometric shapes and motifs
Ralph Lauren	Classic, traditional British styles
Sonia Rykiel	Revolutionary knit styles
Vivien Westwood	Punk and New Wave styles
Yves Saint Laurent	Minimalist, masculine, yet elegant pantsuit style for women, called "Le Smoking"

Sources: Diamond, J., & Diamond, E. (1997). *The world of fashion.* New York: Fairchild Publications; Mendes, V., & de la Haye, E. (1999). *20th century fashion.* New York: Thames & Hudson.

The tempo of change: the fashion cycle

All products, including fashion products, have a finite life cycle. New styles are introduced in the market, last for a certain period of time, decline, and finally disappear. Although the rate and duration of use vary, the diffusion of a specific fashion tends to follow a predictable cycle, called a **fashion cycle** or **fashion life-cycle curve**. The fashion cycle includes four major stages: introduction, growth, maturity, and decline (Easey, 1995) (Figure 1.2). The fashion cycle allows retailers to better predict the sales and profitability of specific styles.

In the **introduction** stage, a new style is introduced to the market and begins to gain acceptance. In this stage, the supply of the new style is limited. For example, in 2009 new bootie styles (short-length boots) were introduced by designer brands, such as Christian Louboutin, to only a few high-price-point boutiques and upscale department stores, such as Neiman Marcus and Saks Fifth Avenue. In this first stage, consumers who were innovative or fashion-conscious and who were willing to pay high prices tried the style.

In the **growth** stage, competition begins to increase as the style is exposed to more and more consumers and gains popularity. Thus, the original bootie styles were modified for mass fashion, which made them available at lower prices. The styles were sold in mid- and high-price-point department stores, such as Macy's, Bloomingdale's, and JCPenney. Sales of the style, marking its acceptance, sharply increased.

The **maturity** stage is usually the longest period in a fashion life cycle. In this stage, competition becomes more intense; therefore, prices begin to drop to appeal

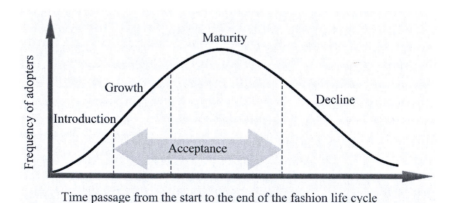

Time passage from the start to the end of the fashion life cycle

Figure 1.2 The fashion life cycle illustrates the rate and duration of consumer acceptance of a specific style.

Source: Adapted from Easey, M. (1995). *Fashion marketing.* Cambridge, MA: Blackwell Science Ltd, p. 129; Solomon, M. R., & Rabolt, N. J. (2009). *Consumer behavior in fashion.* Upper Saddle River, NJ: Pearson Prentice Hall, p. 14.

to the mass market. The bootie styles were modified further as manufacturers used cheaper materials and cheaper labor so that the products could be sold at low prices. In this stage, the styles were also available in discount stores such as Target. The combination of the growth and maturity stages is also called an **acceptance** stage because a large number of consumers accept new styles in this stage (Solomon & Rabolt, 2009).

In the **decline** stage, the styles are going out of fashion and losing their popularity. Sales and profits from the styles rapidly decrease. Retailers that still have the styles put them on sale to eliminate the obsolete stock.

The direction of change: fashion leadership theories

Where do new fashion innovations come from? How do new styles diffuse (i.e., spread) across many different groups of consumers? To answer these questions, three directional fashion theories have been widely used: trickle-down, trickle-across, and trickle-up theories. These theories were developed at various times during the twentieth century, and each theory has been criticized and revised, reflecting the social and market conditions of the times.

The well-known **trickle-down theory** (Figure 1.3) was established by several scholars (e.g., McCracken, 1985; Simmel, 1904; Veblen, 1899). Thorstein Veblen

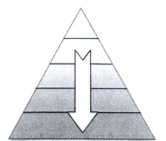

Trickle-down theory
Direction: Downward from elite class to lower classes
Dynamics: Differentiation and imitation; individuality and conformity
Leadership: Upper, elite class

Trickle-across theory
Direction: Horizontal across class
Dynamics: Mass media, fast fashion, fashion ideas in each class
Leadership: Innovators, opinion leaders within subgroups

Trickle-up theory
Direction: Upward from subcultures to elite class
Dynamics: Uniqueness, differentiation from other subcultures and mainstream
Leadership: Subcultures, lower classes

Figure 1.3 Three directional fashion theories, the trickle-up, trickle-across, and trickle-down theories, have been used to explain fashion change and diffusion.
Source: Adapted from Brannon, E. L. (2005). *Fashion forecasting.* New York: Fairchild Publications, pp. 87, 89, 93.

(1899) suggested that fashion change was the result of the need to maintain social stratification. The elite class of his day, dubbed the "**leisure class**" by Veblen, displayed its status and wealth through conspicuous consumption, including ownership of new fashions. The leisure class did not have to work for a living. Instead, it participated in an extravagant lifestyle, including world travel and entertainment. Members were able to access and afford new styles sooner than those in the lower classes; as a result, they were able to symbolize their high status in the social hierarchy. Because there were two distinct social groups during this era, the elite and the lower class, it was relatively simple to explain fashion change; fashion was diffused from the leisure class to the lower classes.

Sociologist Georg Simmel (1904), who was influenced by Veblen's ideas, identified two primary forces of fashion change: **differentiation** and **imitation**. The elite class differentiated itself from the lower classes by adopting new styles. Once these styles were imitated by the lower classes, the elite class gave up the styles and selected new styles in order to maintain its class distinction and superiority. Thus, according to Simmel, fashion change is based on the tendency of the elite class to differentiate itself from the lower classes, reflecting its individuality, and that of the lower classes to imitate the upper class, reflecting their conformity. More recently, Grant McCracken (1985) described the trickle-down theory as an upward **chase and flight** pattern; the lower classes seeks out the status markers of the elite class and tries to obtain these markers for the purpose of imitating the status (chase). When this occurs, the elite class moves on to new styles (flight).

Although this theory has effectively explained why styles are created and subsequently fade, it has been criticized because it oversimplifies our contemporary social system (McCracken, 1985). The trickle-down theory involves only two classes, the upper and the lower, but the social system in which we live today is complex because social classes are created by various factors, such as occupation, education, and income. Also, differentiation and imitation processes simultaneously move not only from upper to lower classes but also within each social class among peers. Another criticism is that the elite class in today's society may not necessarily differentiate itself through fashion to display status. Some even intentionally avoid status symbols (Simon-Miller, 1985). Today's wealthy elite may wear old, ripped jeans and drive a Prius instead of a Rolls-Royce. This is termed "**parody display**," "**reverse ostentation**," or "**conspicuous counterconsumption**" (Brannon, 2010; Solomon & Rabolt, 2009).

The trickle-down theory (Figure 1.3) is useful for predicting fashion change in a society where the upper and lower classes are easily identified. However, King (1963) argued that the trickle-down theory does not sufficiently explain fashion change and behavior. He suggested a competing theory, the "**trickle-across theory**," also called the "**mass-market theory**" or the "**simultaneous-adoption theory**." According to King (1963), new styles trickle across horizontally within classes rather than vertically across classes. Consumers within each class freely choose from a variety of styles, according to their personal taste. Fashion information flows across social classes or groups that share similar life styles and fashion preferences. Consumer acceptance of new styles is most likely to be influenced by fashion leaders, such as innovators (individuals who buy early) and fashion opinion leaders (individuals who are often asked for advice) within a social class.

In modern society, consumers in various social classes are simultaneously exposed to numerous sources of fashion information through mass media and the Internet. Also, fashion companies introduce new fashions at a variety of price points through mass production, which allows consumers in diverse social classes to access new styles at the same time. The diffusion of new styles is accelerated by fast-fashion retailers (e.g., Zara and Forever 21) that introduce less expensive knock-offs of high-fashion designs only a few weeks after they are presented on the runway (Casabona, 2007; Ferdows, Lewis, & Machuca, 2004). Thus, today, consumers are likely to be influenced by fashion leaders within their social class, rather than by those in a higher class. However, this does not mean that the trickle-down theory is useless in explaining fashion change. Many consumers still learn new fashion trends from celebrities and buy fashion items to imitate them.

As discussed, subcultural movements (e.g., "Black Is Beautiful" and hip-hop) have influenced popular culture, including fashion trends. The hippie subculture, originally a youth movement, was prevalent in the United States in the mid-1960s. Hippie styles, such as long hair, peasant blouses, and jeans, largely influenced the fashion of mainstream society. Blue jeans, originally worn by miners and a symbol of laborers, became widely popular as casual clothing styles not only among blue-collar workers and young consumers but also among mainstream consumers.

These examples show that styles do not simply trickle down from the upper classes to the lower. How, then, can we explain the fashion changes of the time? Field (1970) proposed a new theory of fashion, called the "**status float phenomenon**," also known as the "**trickle-up theory**" (Figure 1.3). This theory suggests that upper classes imitate the fashions of the lower classes; new styles or status symbols float up the status pyramid rather than flow down to the lower classes. Subcultures create their own unique styles for the purpose of differentiating themselves from other subcultures and the mainstream (Blumberg, 1975). The styles of subcultures have been important inspiration sources for today's designers and other fashion professionals.

For example, the street fashion "Harajuku" is named for the areas near Harajuku Station in Tokyo, Japan, known for its unique street fashion. It is a place where, every Sunday, young people dressed in various styles, from gothic, rococo, and punk to cute ("Kawaii" in Japanese), gather. Many renowned designers and fashion ideas have sprung from these areas. For example, in 2005, Gwen Stefani, a popular singer, launched the brand Harajuku Lovers, inspired by Japanese pop culture and street fashion. The brand, which includes apparel, perfume, shoes, and fashion accessory lines, is sold in major department stores and cosmetics chain stores (e.g., Sephora). Case 1.1 and 1.2 discuss the history of jeans and the Web site Cool Hunting as examples of the trickle-up theory. Think about examples of each of the trickle-down, trickle-across, and trickle-up theories in Activity 1.1.

CASE 1.1. THE HISTORY OF JEANS (EXAMPLE OF THE TRICKLE-UP THEORY)

Jeans are one example of a fashion that originated within the lower classes and trickled up to mainstream fashion. The history of jeans in the United States started in 1848 with the start of the California Gold Rush. Jeans, called denim at that time, were first worn by miners who needed clothing that was strong and did not tear easily. In 1853 Levi Strauss started a wholesale clothing business in San Francisco and invented blue jeans with Jacob Davis in 1873. Decades later, in the 1930s, Hollywood produced numerous western movies, and jeans became popular with the increase in popularity of cowboys wearing jeans. After World War II, jeans were continuously worn by factory workers, and other jean companies such as Wrangler and Lee began to compete with Levi's in the market. The popularity of jeans after the war was largely influenced by the film and music industries. For instance, James Dean, frequently pictured in jeans, became an iconic figure due in part to his role in Rebel Without a Cause. In the 1960s the term "jeans" was officially adopted by Levi Strauss and Co., and jeans became increasingly popular among university and college students throughout the 1960s and 1970s. The hippie movement led to variations in style, such as embroidered and painted jeans. In the 1980s, for the first time in denim's history, jeans debuted as high-fashion clothing. The term "designer jeans" was coined at that time, and Sergio Valente, Jordache, and Calvin Klein jeans were introduced in the U.S. market. Throughout the 1990s and 2000s, hundreds of new designer-label jeans were created in various price ranges and styles. Jeans remain an important fashion item. Fashion-forward designers such as Chanel, Dior, Chloé, Tom Ford, Gucci, and Versace have presented their own versions of jeans. Also, premium jeans such as 7 for All Mankind, True Religion, and Rock and Republic were introduced to the market, and these jeans have truly become status symbols.

Sources

Blue jeans. (n.d.). Retrieved from http://www.ideafinder.com/history/inventions/blue jeans.htm; Diamond, J., & Diamond, E. (1997). *The world of fashion*. New York: Fairchild Publications; Mendes, V., & de la Haye, E. (1999). *20th century fashion*. New York: Thames and Hudson; The history of jeans. (n.d.). Retrieved from http://www.newint.org/ easier-english/Garment/jhistory.html.

CASE 1.2. COOLHUNTING.COM AS A SOURCE OF INSPIRATION (EXAMPLE OF THE TRICKLE-UP THEORY)

New fashion ideas come from everywhere! Designers search for inspiration from a variety of sources—street fashions, arts, music, architecture, and night spots. Cool Hunting has all of these. Cool Hunting is a Web site introducing unique, updated ideas and products at the intersection of art, design, culture, and technology. Cool Hunting was first published as the personal catalog of Josh Rubin, editor-in-chief, who always seeks creative inspiration and tries to understand the way people do things. Besides serving as an editor of Cool Hunting, Josh also consults on strategy, content, and design for select clients, such as Apple, Google, Adobe, Vodafone, Nike, Microsoft, and MTV. Cool Hunting covers ideas and products from various categories such as furniture, lights, sport equipment, clothing and other fashion-related products, exhibitions, restaurants, indigenous foods, hotels, music, arts, and cultures. The Web site also features weekly videos, showing how artists, designers, and other innovators create their innovations. For instance, the Web site introduces new designers who are creating unique styles inspired by street fashions and pop art. Also, it shows fashion trends and cultural elements of various subcultures. What a great inspirational source for designers! Today, Cool Hunting attracts and inspires more than 500,000 viewers worldwide.

Source

www.coolhunting.com.

ACTIVITY 1.1. FINDING EXAMPLES OF THE TRICKLE-DOWN, TRICKLE-ACROSS, AND TRICKLE-UP THEORIES

Figure 1.3 shows three directional theories of fashion leadership, including the trickle-down, trickle-across, and trickle-up theories. Revisit the section Fashion Trends in Context in this chapter, and identify examples of fashions to which each of these theories—trickle-down, trickle-across, and trickle-up—can be applied. You may find examples from other sources or from your own experiences.

Although these three theories of fashion leadership provide valuable insight into fashion adoption and diffusion, fashion change is considered as a far more complicated process than these theories can explain. To explain today's complex fashion changes, Behling (1985) developed a theory that integrates the components of the trickle-down and trickle-up theories in relation to the median age of the population and the economic health of a country (see Figure 1.4). According to the integrated theory, the median age of the population determines who will be the role models for the majority of people in the society and, consequently, determines the direction of fashion change. When the role models of a society are from an older, more affluent class, fashion change comes from the top to the bottom—it trickles down. On the other hand, when a society is dominated by a younger class, fashion trickles up from the bottom to the top. Also, the speed of the

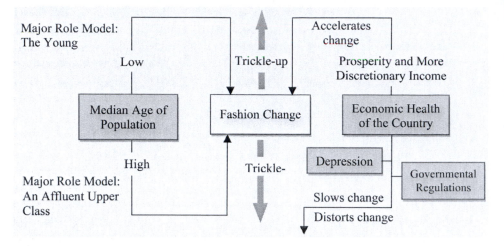

Figure 1.4 The integrated theory model helps explains the complexity of factors influencing to-day's fashion change.

Source: Behling, D. (1985). Fashion change and demographics: A model. *Clothing & Textiles Research Journal,* 4(1), 23.

fashion process is influenced by the amount of disposable or discretionary income; when the economy is good, fashion change speeds up, whereas when the economy is bad, fashion slows.

Recurring fashions

Fashions are born, go through the fashion life cycle, and finally die, like living things. However, after a certain period, some fashions are revived as new fashions. For example, motorcycle leather jackets have been recreated by many designers since they were first introduced in the late 1920s. In the late 2000s, elegant versions of the motorcycle jacket were introduced by designers and contemporary apparel brands (e.g., Alexander McQueen, Vince, and Theory). Leggings are another example. They were outselling jeans in the United States by the early 1990s, but the popularity declined as the pant legs became wider in the late 1990s. In 2005, leggings returned to fashion, and their revival has continued until the late 2000s. Although the basic silhouette of the leggings remains the same, the materials used have varied as technology continues to improve. Recently, leggings made of shiny, metallic, or wet-appearing fabrics have emerged—fashion is evolving. As a final example, Coco Chanel reintroduced the Chanel suit in 1955. In the 1960s, the style was in mass production at various price points. In 1982, the head designer at Chanel, Karl Lagerfeld, reinvented the Chanel suit to be more glamorous and sexy (see Figure 1.5).

One of the earliest fashion theories suggests that fashion change is explained by **shifting erogenous zones**—that different parts of the body are emphasized by veiling

Figure 1.5 This Chanel suit was created by Gabrielle Coco Chanel in 1955. The classic Chanel suit has boxy lines, trim, golden buttons, and a slim skirt lined with a gold link chain (right bottom).
Source: Courtesy of Jean McElvain, Goldstein Museum of Design, College of Design, University of Minnesota.

one part and unveiling another (Laver, 1973). According to Laver, a certain part of the female body is highlighted by a fashion but goes out of fashion when it loses its erotic power due to repeated exposure. Another part, previously unexposed, then becomes the focus of interest. Therefore, erogenous zones shift to maintain interest. Whereas scholars have criticized Laver's theory (e.g., Wilson, 1985) because of its limited applicability to female fashion, the theory points out one of the vital components of fashion change (Brannon, 2010). For example, in the late 1990s and early 2000s, apparel styles were designed to emphasize women's midriffs to reflect consumers' lifestyle changes. Consumers placed great emphasis on fitness and a toned body, particularly a toned stomach or abdomen, which became a status symbol. Think about other examples of erogenous zones in current fashion trends in Activity 1.2.

ACTIVITY 1.2. RECURRING FASHIONS

This chapter discusses the idea that past fashions are important inspirational sources for designers and are renewed and updated from time to time. Can you think of any apparel styles inspired by past fashions? Find five examples of recurring fashions. Also, Laver (1973) explains fashion change by positing a theory of shifting erogenous zones, suggesting that different body parts of women have been covered and uncovered as the points of interest for fashion. Think of current fashion trends. Which part of a woman's body is emphasized in current fashion? Provide three example styles.

Introduction to fashion forecasting terminology

As we have seen throughout this chapter, fashion change is influenced by various factors, such as social, cultural, economic, and technological factors. Therefore, anticipating fashion trends is not a simple task, and forecasters need to consider numerous forces that may affect fashion change. Fashion forecasting is a creative, continual process used to predict the trends of upcoming seasons. It also involves a systematic procedure, including information gathering, market and consumer research, and analysis. Although some fashion companies prefer to research and interpret trends by themselves to keep their originality (Jackson, 2001), major companies are increasingly dependent on trend forecasting and subscribe to materials from more than one forecasting company.

To predict fashion trends, forecasting companies collect information to detect shifts in consumers' ways of living, thinking, and behaving. The staffs of the forecasting companies travel all over the world to observe the art, music, fashion, shopping, and other cultural factors that may influence fashion change. Also, the staffs regularly visit trend-setting cities such as New York, Paris, Milan, London, and Tokyo to provide retail clients with updated fashion information.

Fashion forecasting companies conduct market research to monitor signs of change in the business environment and consumers' purchase behaviors. They look at changes in society, culture, the economy, and technology because fashion trends are often influenced by such changes. As discussed, some events (e.g., the terrorist attacks of September 11, 2001) have directly influenced consumer confidence and fashion adoption and, therefore, retailers' merchandise planning. Fashion forecasting requires an extensive examination of related issues.

Consumer analysis is also an important part of fashion forecasting and includes consumer (market) segmentation, which aims to differentiate types of consumers on the basis of a set of characteristics and behaviors such as age, income, and fashion preferences (Blackwell, Miniard, & Engel, 2001). Consumer analysis allows fashion forecasting companies to examine patterns in consumer characteristics and behaviors. For instance, to anticipate fashion trends for a specific consumer group (e.g., preteen or "tween" consumers), forecasting companies examine level of change in the preteen population, their average disposable income, and their fashion preferences.

Once forecasting companies collect relevant information, they analyze and synthesize it to develop a general direction for a specific season and target markets (e.g., women's, men's, and preteen). Various professionals in the fashion industry use integrated fashion forecasting. For instance, executives and managers may use fashion forecasting to establish long-term marketing strategies, while designers and merchandisers use it to develop products for specific selling seasons. Many fashion companies rely heavily on fashion forecasts. However, although fashion forecasts may help increase the possibility and probability of future success, they are not necessarily the key to success (Brannon, 2010). Fashion retailers also need to consider various aspects of their business, such as target consumers, and the business environment, including competitors.

Historical overview of fashion forecasting

There are few sources that clearly explain the history of fashion forecasting—when, where, and how it was started. The Color Association of the United States (CAUS), originally called the Textile Color Card Association of America (TCCA), founded in 1915, appears to be the first to try to forecast fashion. TCCA issued its first forecast in 1917, focusing on women's fashion. The purpose of fashion forecasting was to suggest colors, organized in groups, to designers and stylists. Since the United States led the world in mass production of clothing after World War II, more specialized fashion forecasting firms emerged in the various industries, including firms that focused on synthetic textiles in the 1950s, menswear in the 1960s, home furnishings in the 1970s, and interior and active wear in the 1980s (Brannon, 2010; McKelvey & Munslow, 2008).

Before the 1960s, fashion moved at a slower pace and was dominated by single trends set by the upper class. Thus, fashion change was adequately explained by the trickle-down theory, and it was easier for forecasters to predict future directions. However, as mass production expanded, various fashion trends from different subcultures developed simultaneously. Advances in information and communication technology have increased the speed of fashion change. As a result of changes in the fashion environment, the role of fashion forecasters has also significantly changed. In the 1960s and 1970s, fashion forecasters were simply fashion spotters, who took pictures and reported what people wore. However, today, this is just one component of their responsibilities. Fashion forecasters focus more on scientific, systematic market analyses, using information collected around the world (McKelvey & Munslow, 2008).

Another significant phenomenon in the field of fashion forecasting today is the boom in online forecasting companies. These companies have revolutionized the industry, offering clients forecasting materials in faster and distinctive ways. For example, many online forecasting companies include a comprehensive online photo archive, containing numerous, up-to-date visual sources from all around the world. Using online forecasting companies, fashion professionals have access to the latest trade fairs and runway shows almost immediately, which saves a significant amount of time and effort for the professionals, who need not travel to fashion cities to look for inspiration every season. Between 1,000 and 1,500 people work as fashion trend forecasters in the industry (Brannon, 2010), and the number is likely to grow with the increased demand for trend information due to growing competition in the fashion industry (Zimmerman, 2008). Fashion professionals realize that "knowing where the market might be heading is obviously a necessary component of staying relevant and on top of the game" (Demasi, 2004, p. 12).

Chapter Summary

- Although terms such as "trend," "style," "design," and "fashion" have been used interchangeably, they have distinct meanings.
- Not all fashions follow a normal life cycle; a short-lived fashion is called a fad, whereas a fashion that lasts an extended period of time is called a classic.
- Fashion change is affected by world events, economic conditions, subcultural influences, social changes, entertainment, technological innovations, and fashion leaders.
- The fashion cycle graphically shows the rate and duration of consumer acceptance of a particular style and consists of four stages: introduction, growth, maturity, and decline.
- Three fashion leadership theories—trickle-down, trickle-across, and trickle-up—have been used to explain the process of fashion change and to identify the leaders in fashion adoption. The integrated theory, combining the trickle-down and trickle-up theories, is used to describe today's complex fashion phenomenon.
- Fashion forecasting is a creative, continual process, involving observation, market and consumer research, analysis, interpretation, and synthesis.

Key Terms

- Chase and flight
- Classic
- Conspicuous consumption
- Continuous innovations
- Counterconsumption
- Design
- Fad
- Fashion
- Fashion cycle
- Fashion life-cycle curve
- High fashion
- Mass market
- Leisure class
- Parody display
- Reverse ostentation
- Shifting erogenous zones
- Simultaneous-adoption theory
- Status float phenomenon
- Style
- Trend
- Trickle-across theory
- Trickle-down theory
- Trickle-up theory

Questions for review and discussion

1. Identify the differences among a fad, a fashion, and a classic. What are the three most popular styles in current fashion? Are they fads, fashions, or classics?
2. Which fashion leadership theories do you think best describes the origins and processes of the fashions you identified in discussion question one?
3. Who are the observable fashion elites these days? How do they influence mass consumers? Are there any styles that became popular because of the fashion elites?
4. What is the latest innovation these days? You may think of some examples in areas other than apparel, such as computers, cell phones, cars, or Web sites. What stages of the fashion cycle do you think they are in? Provide your justification.
5. Some people say forecasting makes fashion narrow and boring because designers introduce similar styles based on the fashion trends of the season. Do you agree that forecasters plot the next fashion trend, resulting in fashion generalization? Why or why not?

Suggested Reading

Veblen, T. (1899). *The theory of the leisure class.* New York: Macmillan.

References

Anderson, C., & Cornwell, R. L. (1977). "Black is beautiful" and the color preferences of Afro-American youth. *Journal of Negro Education, 46*(1), 76–88.

Behling, D. (1985). Fashion change and demographics: A model. *Clothing & Textiles Research Journal, 4,* 18–24.

Blackwell, R. D., Miniard, P. W., & Engel, J. F. (2001). *Consumer behavior.* Troy, MO: Harcourt College Publishers.

Blue jeans. (n.d.). Retrieved from http://www.ideafinder.com/history/inventions/bluejeans.htm

Blumberg, P. (1975). The decline and fall of the status symbol: Some thoughts on status in a post-industrial society. *Social Problems, 21*(4), 480–497.

Blume, L. M. M. (2008). High styles for low times. Retrieved from http://www.slate.com/id/2191398/

Brannon, E. L. (2010). *Fashion forecasting* (3rd ed.). New York: Fairchild Books.

Casabona, L. (2007, July 23). Retailer Forever 21 facing a slow of design lawsuits. *Women's Wear Daily,* p. 194.

Davies, C. B. (Ed.) (2008). *Encyclopedia of the African diaspora: Origin, experiences and culture* (Vol. 1) (pp. 493–495). Santa Barbara, CA: ABC-CLIO, Inc.

Demasi, L. (2004, March 4). Cool hunting. *Sydney Morning Herald* (Australia), p. 12.

Diamond, J., & Diamond, E. (1997). *The world of fashion.* New York: Fairchild Publications.

Easey, M. (1995). *Fashion marketing.* Cambridge, MA: Blackwell Science Ltd.

Ferdows, K., Lewis, M. A., & Machuca, J. A. D. (2004, November). Rapid-fire fulfillment. *Harvard Business Review, 82*(11), 104–110.

Field, G. A. (1970). The status float phenomenon—the upward diffusion of innovation. *Business Horizons, 8,* 45–52.

The history of jeans. (n.d.). Retrieved from http://www.newint.org/easier-english/Garment/jhistory.html

Jackson, T. (2001). The process of fashion trend development leading to a season. In E. Hines & M. Bruce (Eds.), *Fashion marketing: Contemporary issue*. Jordan Hill, Oxford, UK: Butterworth Heinemann.

King, C. W. (1963). A rebuttal to the "trickle down" theory. In S. A. Greyer (Ed.), *Towards scientific marketing* (pp. 108–125). Chicago: American Marketing Association.

Laver, J. (1973). Taste and fashion since the French Revolution. In G. Wills & D. Midgley (Eds.), *Fashion marketing* (pp. 379–389). London: George Allen: Irwin.

McCracken, G. (1985). The trickle-down theory revisited. In M. R. Solomon (Ed.), *The psychology of fashion* (pp. 39–54). Lexington, MA: Lexington Books.

McKelvey, K., & Munslow, J. (2008). *Fashion forecasting*. West Sussex, UK: Wiley-Blackwell.

Mendes, V., & de la Haye, E. (1999). *20th century fashion*. New York: Thames & Hudson.

The power suit. (n.d.). International Museum of Women. Retrieved from http://www.imow.org/wpp/stories/viewStory?storyId=926

Savage, J. (2001). *England's dream: Anarchy, sex pistols, punk rock, and beyond*. New York: St. Martin's Griffin.

Simmel, G. (1904). Fashion. *International Quarterly, 10,* 130–155.

Simon-Miller, F. (1985). Commentary: Signs and cycles in the fashion system. In M. R. Solomon (Ed.), *The psychology of fashion system* (pp. 71–81). Lexington, MA: Lexington Books/D. C. Health.

Solomon, M. R., & Rabolt, N. J. (2009). *Consumer behavior in fashion*. Upper Saddle River, NJ: Pearson Prentice Hall.

Sproles, G. B., & Burns, L. D. (1994). *Changing appearances: Understanding dress in contemporary society* (pp. 122–136). New York: Fairchild Publications.

Stone, E. (2008). *The dynamics of fashion*. New York: Fairchild Books.

Ten most popular haircuts of all time. (2010, June 3). Retrieved from http://shine.yahoo.com/channel/beauty/10-most-popular-haircuts-of-all-time-1632425/

Terrorism's trauma casts a dark shadow over luxury sector. (2001, October 25). *Women's Daily News,* p. 1.

Veblen, T. (1899). *The theory of the leisure class*. New York: Macmillan.

Weedon, C. (2002). Key issues in postcolonial feminism—a western perspective. *Gender Forum: An International Journal of Gender Studies*. Retrieved from http://www.genderforum.org/issues/genderealisations/key-issues-in-postcolonial-feminism-a-western-perspective/

Wilbekin, E. (1999). Great aspirations: Hip hop and fashion dress for excess and success. In A. Light (Ed.), *The vibe history of hip hop* (pp. 277–284). New York: Three Rivers Press.

Wilson, E. (1985). *Adorned in dreams*. Berkeley: University of California Press.

Zimmerman, E. (2008, May 11). Roaming the world, detecting fashion. *The New York Times,* p. 14.

2

CONSUMERS' ROLE
IN FASHION ADOPTION

Objectives

* Understand the stages of the innovation adoption process
* Understand how attributes of the innovation and personal characteristics of consumers affect the rate of adoption of an innovation
* Understand how fashion firms can use their knowledge of factors affecting the rate of adoption to develop successful development, merchandising, and marketing practices

As noted in chapter 1, each new product or trend introduced to the market has a life cycle that begins with its introduction, then goes through the growth and maturity stages where the product is adopted by a segment of consumers, all followed by the product's decline when it falls out of favor (Gorchels, 2005; Sproles, 1981). (New products or trends are referred to as innovations in the present chapter.) This cycle can transform gradually (fashion products), steadily (classic products), or swiftly (fads). In each case, *consumers* go through the stages of the innovation adoption process, but at different rates. The present chapter identifies (a) the stages of the innovation adoption process, (b) five perceived attributes of an innovation that affect its rate of adoption by consumers, and (c) personal characteristics of the consumer that affect the rate of adoption as well. The chapter also includes a discussion of strategies that fashion firms may use to facilitate the adoption of a fashion innovation.

The innovation adoption process

Think about the first time you heard or saw a new trend, such as the military or warrior trend, which gained popularity in 2010 (Figure 2.1). Perhaps there were elements in a few collections during February and March fashion weeks that began to register for you as the warrior trend (awareness), such as Donatella Versace's metallic-breastplate-inspired details on the bust of a dress; Balmain's tunic dresses with shoulder epaulettes, inspired by ancient Roman soldiers; Balenciaga's gladiator-inspired urban tunics with plating; or Rick Owens's loincloth-style skirts and spiked gold cuffs. Next, you began to look for other examples of the trend (interest) when surfing fashion Web sites in April, then came to the conclusion that you liked the details of the trend (evaluation), began trying on warrior-inspired products such as leather tunics (trial) during May shopping trips, and ended your shopping sojourn with the purchase and use (adoption) of warrior-inspired sandals (Figure 2.2) in June. You have just moved through Beal, Rogers, and Bohlen's (1957) five stages of the **innovation adoption process model.** Rural sociologists (Beal et al., 1957) originally used this model to explain the process of adoption of farm practices (e.g., the use of a new corn hybrid), but the model is equally relevant to the adoption process for innovations in consumer products and fashion trends, as just illustrated.

Looking at these five stages, we find that the process begins with the **awareness stage.** In this stage, the consumer becomes aware of some new offering, such as an idea, product, or trend. Little may be known about the new offering, and consumers may lack detail about the offering, but they are aware of its existence. In the

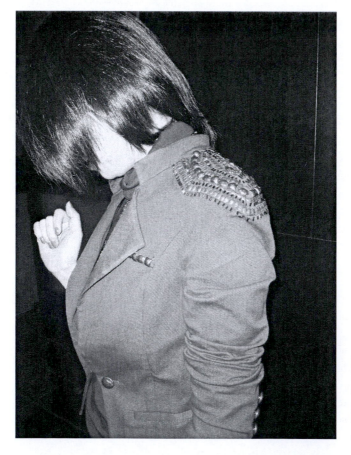

Figure 2.1 The military influence is evident in the shoulder epaulette and breast pocket details, as well as the U.S. army green color.
Source: Ann Marie Fiore.

Figure 2.2 Shoe designs inspired by ancient Roman gladiator footwear.
Source: Ann Marie Fiore.

interest stage, the consumer's curiosity is piqued, leading to efforts to gather more information about the new offering. The consumer begins to wonder if the offering is right for her or suits her needs. In the evaluation stage, the consumer processes the gathered information and mentally "tries on" the new offering for her own situation. For instance, the consumer may ask, "Would this work with what I already own?" or "Does this trend work for someone my age?"

In the trial stage, the consumer physically tests the new offering to see if reality matches her expectations. For a fashion trend, the consumer may try products on in the store to see if the style is flattering and comfortable. In the case of the sandals, the visual truncation of the leg (i.e., making the legs look shorter and wider) may lead the customer to reject the trend during the in-store trial stage, or the shoes may be purchased and shown to friends who define the shoes as hideous. Back they go to the store, and the new offering is rejected. If friends evaluate the shoes positively, the consumer may move on to the final stage of the model, the adoption stage, in which case the consumer concludes that she likes the new trend and wears the shoes during the summer season and possibly into the fall with another trend of the season, knee-high socks.

Individuals may go through the **stages of the adoption process model** at different rates, depending on the **attributes of the innovation** and the characteristics of the individual consumer (Rogers, 2003). The present section focuses on (a) how attributes of the innovation may affect its rate of adoption and (b) how fashion firms may use this knowledge to develop practices that facilitate consumers' movement through the adoption process.

According to Rogers (2003), there are five perceived attributes of an innovation that affect its rate of adoption. The first attribute is **relative advantage**, which is defined as "the degree to which an innovation is perceived as better than the idea it supersedes" (Rogers, 2003, p. 229). According to Rogers, the greater the perceived relative advantage of an innovation, the more rapid its rate of adoption. He noted that an innovation can provide an economic and/or status-related advantage. In addition, relative advantage may come from aesthetic, functional (e.g., health-related), physical (comfort-related), psychological (e.g., self-esteem-related), and time-saving benefits of the innovation. (see Fiore, 2010, for a discussion of benefits from apparel products.)

Consider the relative advantage of jersey knit leggings over jeans. Leggings may be less expensive than jeans, particularly if we compare nonbranded leggings to popular brands of jeans such as 7 for All Mankind, Citizens of Humanity, or True Religion. Thus, leggings may provide a perceived economic advantage, but, because they do not have the status of the clearly branded jeans, the relative advantage of leggings may be diminished, which could slow the rate of adoption of the trend. Leggings may be seen as offering functional, time-saving, and physical benefits, because they are easily tucked into boots, they dry quickly after washing, and the knit fabrics is comfortable. Yet, leggings may be seen as lacking in the area of psychological benefit, because leggings do not have the positive symbolic meaning of jeans for young consumers.

Whereas a firm may believe it is building certain benefits into an innovation, the relative advantage may differ for different consumers. For instance, variation in level of fashion consciousness and innovativeness among Korean consumers was associated with differences in their perception of aesthetic, economic, health, and uniqueness benefits offered by fragranced textile products (i.e., impregnating fabric with tiny cells of fragrance that open when abraded, similar to the technology used to create scent strips) (Yoh, 2005).

To facilitate the adoption of an innovation by consumers, a fashion firm may alter current options to create new products that provide a relative advantage. For instance, consider the proliferation of the innovation denim leggings (a.k.a., "jeggings"), which consumers may perceive as having the relative advantage of comfort offered by leggings added to the status and psychological advantage of jeans. In fact, excellent quarterly growth for Joez Jeans was attributed to the rapid consumer acceptance of the company's denim leggings ("Joez jeans," 2010).

The second attribute of an innovation is **compatibility**, which is "the degree to which an innovation is perceived as being consistent with the existing values, past experiences, and needs of potential adopters" (Rogers, 2003, p. 240). Consumers judge innovations against previously accepted ideas. When the innovation is seen as consistent with such ideas or seems familiar, it is assumed that adoption of the new offering will be accelerated. Thus, the adoption of the innovation of denim leggings may have been accelerated because of consumers' past experience; they look similar in cut to the widely accepted "skinny jeans."

Considering compatibility may also help the fashion firm accelerate adoption of an innovation. For instance, Chinese luxury fashion brands, new to China, are incorporating traditional design details to attract Chinese consumers (H. Tao [Wuhan Textile University design faculty], personal communication, October 18, 2010) (Figures 2.3a–b).

The name of an innovation may affect its perceived familiarity or compatibility with existing values (Rogers, 2003). The phrase "denim legging" may make the consumer feel comfortable with the innovative product because these terms are familiar and positively evaluated. Consumers within Western culture value youth, which is associated with denim, and value comfort, which is associated with leggings. Sending offers related to denim leggings to those who have purchased skinny jeans may be more effective than sending the same offers to consumers who prefer looser styles, because the skinny-jeans consumer may see similarities with her existing values (e.g., the thinness of her body) and past experience (e.g., preference for the lean garment silhouette).

The third attribute, **complexity**, is "the degree to which an innovation is perceived as difficult to understand and use" (Rogers, 2003, p. 257). More complex innovations are assumed to experience a slower rate of adoption. This attribute may not be as important as relative advantage or compatibility to the adoption of fashion products, because these products are usually not hard to understand or use. However, with the addition of nanotechnology to apparel that have medical applications ("Nanotechnology," n.d.), complexity may become a bigger issue.

The fourth attribute is **trialability**, which is "the degree to which an innovation may be experimented with on a limited basis" (Rogers, 2003, p. 258). If a consumer can easily try an innovation, it enhances speed of adoption. Trialability is particularly important to those who are first to adopt an innovation, because they do not have peers who have already adopted the innovation (Rogers, 2003).

Firms may offer various forms of trialability. Fashion firms allow limited trialability when the consumer tries on products in fitting rooms or through virtual models (i.e., virtual images of the consumer's body form wearing the product), but trialability should take place in the actual use situation. For examples, firms may use experiential marketing events; thus, Patagonia set up a climbing wall at a sporting competition where consumers could try out innovative climbing gear. Whereas cosmetics firms provide trial size samples and free makeovers in the season's new color palette, Chanel goes a step further. Its makeup studios in Dubai's Mall of the

Figure 2.3 a–b Some modern Chinese fashion (a) takes its inspiration from the qipao (pronounced chi pow), a traditional form of Chinese dress still worn today for weddings (b).

Sources: 2.3a, Ann Marie Fiore; 2.3b, Courtesy of Wei-Chen Chen.

Emirates allow the consumer to see how she will look under lighting conditions encountered in actual use situations (e.g., day or evening lighting) by incorporating a new ceiling lighting system (DiNardo, 2007).

The final attribute of an innovation is **observability.** This is "the degree to which the results of an innovation are visible to others" (Rogers, 2003, p. 258). The easier it is for others to see the innovation adopted by a consumer, the more rapid its adoption. The observability of the mobile phone likely affected its rapid rate of adoption around the world; consumer use of the phone is very public, from both a visual and an (annoyingly) auditory standpoint (Rogers, 2003).

Fashion firms may enhance observability through **product placement** in the media, such as arranging for branded products to show up as props in films, TV shows, video games, and even news programs (Pilkington, 2008). Products may move from being props to becoming integral to the story line of a TV show episode (e.g., *30 Rock* and Diet Snapple; Nussbaum, 2008); this is called **product integration.** Fashion firms give complementary products to celebrities in the hope that they will wear or twitter about the innovation and thereby spark interest among consumers. What question is always asked of the celebrity on the red carpet? "Who are you wearing?"

Celebrities are no longer the main outlets for endorsements. Fashion firms are now sending their innovations to bloggers in the hope that they will be positively reviewed on the blogger's site. Consumer product firms are using fans found on the brand's Facebook site as endorsers of innovations among their friends and family. This endorser may receive products to use as an incentive with friends and family, which reinforces trust in the endorsement. These are just some of the ways to increase observability. Case 2.1 illustrates how the popularity of the innovative designs of a fashion merchandiser turned floral designer, known for her fabric-covered "box" of flowers, were helped by observability.

CASE 2.1. ISU GRAD IS "FLORIST TO THE STARS"

Whereas Harry Winston may be considered the jeweler to the stars, Kimm Birkicht may be considered the "florist to the stars". Birkicht has a floral-design studio in Hollywood with the name, "The Velvet Garden". Included on its mailing list are entertainment high society members such as Sharon Stone and Jennifer Garner, whose weddings Birkicht glamourized. However, this esteemed professional position is quite a distance from where Birkicht started—sweeping the floors for a florist. Before the entrée into the world of floral design, she was a 1980 graduate of Iowa State University who then spent eight years working as a visual merchandiser for Neiman Marcus.

During this stint at Neiman Marcus, she admired the work of a particular florist, which may explain why she incorporated flowers with various props, backdrops, and fashion when she created window and other store displays. "I really admired that natural element, and I just loved this florist's work," Birkicht said. Birkicht went to the florist with a modest offer; she would start at the bottom and do anything needed, including sweeping the floors, if he would mentor her. Through working with him and watching him, she learned about every aspect of the floral business, not just the beautiful, fragrant bouquet side of the business. She learned about marketing, client meetings and paperwork, and the need to do no small amount of floor sweeping. "We fly in flowers from all over the world and it's a big project just getting them in the door."

When she started out, most of Birkicht's clientele were stylists and designers who really liked her work. A big break, she was hired to do the flowers for the set of the "Ellen" show. Things began to snowball; stylists sent bouquets to their movie star clients, people noticed The Velvet Garden's name in the credits of "Ellen", and she began to get written up in magazines like Vogue and Architectural Digest. These events enhanced the observability of her designs and led to Jennifer Aniston showing up and becoming one of Birkicht's best clients. As you will see in the next section, having fashion leaders such as stylists, designers, and famous actors including Jennifer Aniston give their "stamp of approval" to the Velvet Garden, may have facilitated rate of adoption of the new floral designs.

"She's been very loyal to me, and I'm very honored to have her as a client. She's very sweet and sends lots of flowers to her friends," Birkicht said. Birkicht's signature design is her fabric-covered "box" of flowers, and many of her designs involve fabric. "When I was trying to come up with a name for my business," Birkicht says, "I kept going back to things from my fashion background and about flowers in a fabric setting. And I thought about the lushness of velvet."

Source

Miller, J. (2010, May 15). ISU grad is "florist to the stars." *DesMoinesRegister.com*. Retrieved from http://www.desmoinesregister.com/apps/pbcs.dll/article?AID=20105150301

Factors influencing the rate of adoption: Consumer adopter categories

In the previous section, we showed how the attributes of the innovation affect its rate of adoption. As noted, a fashion firm may employ various practices to move consumers through the adoption process, but two consumers exposed to the same practices will likely move through at different paces because of their personal characteristics. The present section illustrates how consumers are categorized into segments according to the rate at which they adopt an innovation. The categories of adopters are innovators, early adopters, early majority, late majority, and laggards (referred to as late adopters to avoid the negative connotations associated with the term "laggard") (Rogers, 2003).

The next three subsections focus on fashion change agents: innovators, early adopters, and opinion leaders (i.e., market mavens), because most of the literature focuses on these change agents and because they are particularly important to launching a successful innovation. Figure 2.4 shows the approximate distribution of adopters in the different categories.

Innovators: Characteristics, motivations, and roles

Innovators are the first individuals to adopt an innovation. They may even be the creators of the innovation when trends begin on the streets. They make up only a small percentage (2.5%) of all those who adopt a new product or innovation. They are characterized as colorful, contemporary, indulgent, venturesome, rash, daring, and risk takers (Phau & Lo, 2004; Rogers, 2003). DeeDee Gordon, a marketing consultant to the advertising firm for the Converse and Airwalk brands, described innovators:

> These are kids who are outcasts in some way. It does not matter whether it's actually true. They feel that way. They pick up on bigger-picture things, whereas the mainstream kids think about being overweight . . . or how they are doing in school. You see more activists in trendsetters. People with more passion . . . somebody who is an individual, who definitely sets herself apart from everybody else, who doesn't look like her peers. (Gladwell, 2002, p. 208)

In terms of consumer behavior, innovators tend to buy new products sooner than other consumers (Midgely & Dowling, 1978) and tend to switch to new

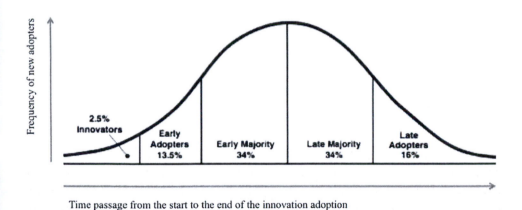

Time passage from the start to the end of the innovation adoption

Figure 2.4   Rogers's Innovation Adopter Categories.
Source: Adapted from Rogers, E. M. (2003). *Diffusion of innovations* (4th ed.). New York: Free Press, p. 281.

products and brands rather than remain with their previous choices (Steenkamp, ter Hofstede, & Wedel, 1999). Consumers with a high level of innovativeness may be motivated by the desire for new and different *experiences*, rather than new product acquisition. These consumers have been shown to be motivated not only by a need for novelty and uniqueness but also by the enjoyment they derive from evaluating information, discovering facts, and examining product attributes (Engelland, Hopkins, & Larson, 2001).

Innovators frequently are young and well educated, have the financial resources to easily absorb financial loss, are very social, are in close contact with sources of product innovations, and interact with other innovators (Rogers, 2003). According to Behling (1992), fashion innovators have been found to read more fashion magazines, spend more time seeking information about fashion trends, belong to more organizations, and be more gregarious and self-confident than noninnovators (Painter & Pinegar, 1971; Reynolds & Darden, 1973). They also tend to make impulse purchases (Phau & Lo, 2004).

Innovativeness has been tied to **opinion leadership** in the United States (Hirschman & Adcock, 1978) and in European and Asian countries (Ruvio & Shoham, 2007; Schrank, Sugawara, & Kim, 1982). Opinion leadership is defined as "the degree to which an individual is able to influence other individuals' attitudes or overt behavior informally in a desired way . . . [and] is not a function of an individual's formal position" (Rogers, 2003, p. 27). We discuss opinion leadership further in the chapter.

Innovators may be identified by their behaviors, such as actual adoption of new products (Im, Bayus, & Mason, 2003), relative time of adoption for a particular product (Im, Mason, & Houston, 2007; Midgley & Dowling, 1978), and purchase intentions (Holak & Lehmann, 1990). Conversely, innovators may be identified by their responses to questions in developed scales, such as consumer innovativeness scales, which measure receptivity to new experiences and novel stimuli (Goldsmith, 1984) or by their tendency to buy new and different products instead of sticking to previous choices (Steenkamp et al., 1999). Research (Citrin, Sprott, Silverman, & Stem, 2000; Goldsmith, Freiden, & Eastman, 1995; Im et al., 2003) suggests that innovativeness may be domain specific, which means that a consumer may be an innovator when it comes to a specific product category such as fashion apparel but not for other categories, such as electronic equipment or fishing gear.

Innovators play an important role in the diffusion process; they introduce innovations. For instance, an innovator may wear a bold cape from Uzbekistan to a party, which increases her friends' interest in fashion capes, a trend in 2010. Therefore, innovators are often the source of new ideas for the group. Because they are frequently opinion leaders, their advice is valued and influences the thoughts and behaviors of other consumers. Thus, innovators are the "spark" for a new trend or innovation, which ignites the interest of other early adopters.

Fashion firms in the development stage of a fashion innovation may want to assemble a panel of innovators to provide initial ideas. Case 2.2, illustrates how innovators have been used to spark new ideas. These panels may also be used in assessment of innovation prototypes. Questions about whether the innovator will adopt a fashion innovation, the perceived potential success of the innovation among consumers, and the changes needed for the innovation to be successful can help the firm launch a winning innovation.

CASE 2.2. TRANSLATING TRENDS BETWEEN INNOVATORS AND EARLY MAJORITY CONSUMERS

Airwalk, an athletic shoe and apparel company, wanted to expand its market from skateboarder (innovators) to the mainstream (early majority) market. It hired Lambesis, an advertising firm, to help with this process. The first thing that Lambesis did was to gather information from innovators that the firm would then translate for the mainstream market through Airwalk advertising. A network of young innovators in major cities, including Chicago, London, New York, and Tokyo, was created. Two or three times a year marketing expert DeeDee Gordon asked the innovators about music listened to and television shows watched, clothing purchased, and goals and aspirations.

Gordon then identified new trends that jumped from innovators to mainstream consumers three months to a year later. The new trends that were popular among innovators across the different cities became the concepts for the development of ads. For instance, interest in kung fu movies was translated into a kung fu parody ad in which an Airwalk-wearing teen fights off martial art villains with a skateboard. These ads translated the interests of innovators into a language understandable by early majority consumers, which helped increase the sale of Airwalk products to a mainstream market.

However, within three years the company's sales began to decline, because innovators lost interest in the brand. There were a few reasons for the decline. The brand began to lose the cutting-edge reputation created by its inventive product designs. Instead of listening to the innovators, the company listened to the sales staff, which resulted in an indistinctive, mainstream look that was unappealing to innovators. Airwalk eliminated its segmentation strategy where small, independent, core skate shops received exclusive product lines while mall stores received different product lines. The independent skate shops were no longer given unique, more durable products with better materials, padding, cushioning systems, and expensive uppers. Thus, innovators were no longer able to buy an exclusive shoe; the same indistinctive styles were available to consumers everywhere. Innovators no longer thought the brand was cool, and it lost its following among innovators.

Source
Gladwell, M. (2002). *The tipping point: How little things can make a big difference.* New York: Little, Brown and Co.

Fashion firms in the process of releasing innovations may want to identify fashion innovators on the basis of past consumer patterns. New technology (e.g., "Finding profit-driving customers," 2010) that allows retailers to easily find associations among consumer buying patterns from in-store or Web site sales data may identify those who are the first to adopt new trends. For instance, this new technology may be used to identify consumers who are among the first to purchase SKUs associated with new trends introduced to the sales floor or Web site. Once such early adopters have been identified, the fashion firm may send them notifications that emphasize the release date of the innovation (e.g., the season's new product lines).

Goldsmith, Flynn, and Goldsmith (2003) emphasize that consumers with a high level of innovativeness should be the target of marketing efforts, as they have a thirst for knowledge, are typically less price sensitive than other consumers, and more likely to be heavy product users. Special promotions for innovators may accelerate awareness and evaluation of the new trends among potential consumers, who may share their finds with other consumers through actual behavior (i.e., wearing the new trend) or by word of mouth. Because innovators are willing to pay full price for new products, like to interact with other innovators, and relish the sense of uniqueness (Steenkamp et al., 1999) that comes with possessing something others do not, these promotions may be most effective if they take the form of special, invitation-only events for innovators, rather than monetary discounts.

Experiential shopping environments that offer new and sensory-rich shopping venues as well as hands-on evaluation and exploration of new and unique products may attract consumers with a high level of innovativeness. These environments provide opportunities for direct interaction and engagement with an innovation, which not only provides desired stimulation but also aids in more functional aspects of product evaluation (Kim, Fiore, Niehm, & Jeong, 2010).

Now that you have a basic understanding of innovators, try Activity 2.1. This activity will give you a chance to explore your level of consumer innovativeness towards fashion. Try to be as truthful as possible; we would all like to believe we are fashion innovators, but only a small percentage of consumers are actually innovators.

ACTIVITY 2.1. MEASURING YOUR CONSUMER INNOVATIVENESS TOWARD FASHION

Consumers vary in level of innovativeness. The following scale is useful in identifying one's tendency toward fashion innovativeness. Each member of the class should record his or her responses to the questions below by circling the number that best describes his or her level of agreement with the statement. There are no right or wrong answers. Once all responses are recorded, each person can find his or her total by adding the numbers circled.

As a class, create three groups. One group should have those with scores closest to 49. The second group should have those closest to 7. The third group should include those in the middle range of scores. Now compare the appearance of members in the first two groups. Are there discernable differences between the two groups in terms of innovativeness of appearance? What are the noticeable differences? (If this is a fashion course, there may be less variety in appearance than is usually found in a general education class.)

Ask each member to record how many times per week he or she checks out Web sites related to fashion or the retail industry. Average the number within each group by totaling the number from each member and dividing by the number of members of the group. Which group had the highest average, representing a higher level of information gathering about fashion?

Within each group, come up with a list of at least five fashion firm strategies that you think would be most effective in getting you to adopt a new trend. Are there differences in the strategies suggested by the three groups? If so, what are they?

Table A2.1

Consumer Innovativeness toward Fashion*	Strongly Disagree						Strongly Agree
1. I often seek out information about new fashion products, trends, and brands.	1	2	3	4	5	6	7
2. I like to go to places where I will be exposed to information about new fashion products, trends and brands.	1	2	3	4	5	6	7
3. I like magazines that introduce new fashion products, trends, and brands.	1	2	3	4	5	6	7
4. I frequently look for new fashion products and services.	1	2	3	4	5	6	7
5. I seek out situations in which I will be exposed to new and different sources of fashion products and trend information.	1	2	3	4	5	6	7
6. I am continually seeking new fashion product experiences.	1	2	3	4	5	6	7
7. I take advantage of the first available opportunity to find out about new and different fashion products and trends.	1	2	3	4	5	6	7

*This scale was adapted from the consumer innovativeness scale found in Manning, K. C., Bearden, W. O., & Madden, T. J. (1995). Consumer innovativeness and the adoption process. *Journal of Consumer Psychology, 4*(4), 329–345.

Innovators and early adopters, as change agents, want revolutionary change and want to be set apart from the majority of consumers (Gladwell, 2002). **Early adopters** are the second fastest category of individuals to adopt an innovation, but they still make up a small percentage (13.5%) of consumers who adopt an innovation. They are not perceived as outcasts, as innovators may be. Instead, they are an integral part of a (digital and/or face-to-face) social network.

Early adopters are typically higher in socioeconomic status and education level than late adopters. They are also less dogmatic (i.e., less likely to hold rigid opinions); have a greater ability to deal with abstractions, uncertainty, and risk; have greater intelligence; have a more favorable attitude toward change; and have a greater sense of self-efficacy (i.e., control over one's destiny) (Rogers, 2003). Moreover, in comparison to late adopters, early adopters are more socially active; more frequently communicate with individuals from and travel to places outside their local community; have greater exposure to media channels (e.g., magazines, blogs); and have greater knowledge of innovations.

Early adopters play an interesting role in the diffusion process. They make the trends started by innovators more palatable to mainstream consumers. One way early adopters do this is by translating the trend into a form more acceptable to mainstream consumers. DeeDee Gordon, a marketing consultant, illustrates the role of early adopters: "They see what the weird kids are doing and they tweak it. They start doing it themselves, but they change it a bit. They make it more usable. . . . They look at it and say, it's a little off. But there is a way I can change it and make it okay" (Gladwell, 2002, pp. 200–201).

Another way to make the innovation more palatable is by reducing the perceived risk associated with its adoption. **Perceived risk** is the collection of negative or unexpected consequences a consumer fears may occur as a result of a purchase decision (Toffler & Imber, 2000). Perceived risk may take a number of forms, including functional risk (e.g., "Will this product wear well over time?") and social risk (e.g., "What will my friends say about me if I wear this?"). Perceived risk may be reduced by communication between early adopters and early majority consumers. For instance, brand representatives (early adopters) may provide evidence of satisfactory product quality and of growing demand for an innovation by other consumers in the same demographic group.

If innovators are the "spark," then early adopters are the "kindling" used to ignite a trend among early majority consumers. A trend is partially ignited through communication between early adopters, as opinion leaders, and early majority consumers. Early adopters have the highest degree of opinion leadership among adopter categories (Rogers, 2003). They are frequently both very knowledgeable about the product category and good communicators (Gladwell, 2002). They are respected by a large group of consumers, which is not usually true for innovators. Early adopters are perceived by the mainstream consumer to be successful in making the right calls on new innovations and put their stamp of approval on the innovation by actually using it. Therefore, early adopters become role models with whom many other consumers will check or observe before they too decide to adopt a new trend (Rogers, 2003).

Market mavens: Characteristics, motivations, and roles

Early adopters, unlike market mavens, are purchasers or users of the product or service. However, market mavens are important change agents, because of their opinion leadership. **Market mavens** are "individuals who have information about many kinds of products, places to shop, and other facets of markets, and initiate discussions with consumers and respond to requests from consumers for market information" (Feick & Price, 1987, p. 85). Like opinion leaders, market mavens enjoy talking about products, but opinion leaders focus on a specific product category (Feick & Price, 1987). Moreover, market mavens are diffusers not only of product information but also of marketing mix information (e.g., cheapest price, stores carrying a product, best service) (Chelminski & Coulter, 2007; Feick & Price, 1987; Slama & Williams, 1990).

Market mavens are said to be socially motivated; they receive great pleasure from helping others (Gladwell, 2002). Their knowledge, social skills, and lack of ulterior motive in their desire to help, augments their impact on the attitude and behavior of consumers. Market mavens are seen as having a stronger influence than opinion leaders in the marketplace (Feick & Price, 1987; Goldsmith et al., 2003), confirming the value of understanding the relationship between market maven tendencies and innovation diffusion.

Market mavens are value conscious (Engelland et al., 2001). Because they like to help, they distribute coupons and take friends shopping (Gladwell, 2002). This suggests that incentive programs that provide coupons to share via e-mail or multiple paper coupons may be effective; if the market maven uses one coupon, he or she still has other coupons to share. Market mavenism has been connected with shopping for enjoyment (Wiedmann, Walsh, & Mitchell, 2001) and with the need for uniqueness (Clark & Goldsmith, 2005). This suggests the importance of creating unique, engaging retail experiences and of gearing promotions to market mavens when launching innovations. Market mavens contribute greatly to consumer word-of-mouth communications (Wangenheim, 2005), which makes cultivating and pleasing market mavens important for smaller firms that are heavily dependent on word-of-mouth communication rather than large advertising budgets.

Research shows that market mavens can be found in countries around the world, including Germany, Israel, Poland, South Africa, and the United States (Ruvio & Shoham, 2007). According to Linda Price, a marketing professor, about 50 percent of the U.S. population knows someone who matches the market maven description (Gladwell, 2002, p. 62). To close this section, complete Activity 2.2, which will help you identify the market mavens in your midst.

ACTIVITY 2.2. IDENTIFYING THE MARKET MAVENS IN OUR MIDST

According to one marketing professor, about half the U.S. population knows a market maven, or an individual who has "information about many kinds of products, places to shop, and other facets of markets, and initiates discussions with consumers and responds to requests from consumers for market information" (Feick & Price, 1987, p. 85). Determine if there is anyone who fits the description in your personal life. Describe how the individual has characteristics, motives, and behaviors similar to those that characterize a market maven.

To determine if there are market mavens within the group of students in the class, each student should record his or her responses to the questions below by circling the number that best describes his or her level of agreement with each statement. There are no right or wrong answers. Once all responses are recorded, students can find their total by adding the numbers circled.

Identify those who have the highest scores, with the highest possible score being 35. (Scores above 30 suggest strong market maven tendencies.) Ask the high scorers to list the product categories for which they have a lot of information and would give advice to others. Are there a variety of product categories for each high scorer? What does that say? Are they opinion leaders or market mavens?

Determine whether those with the highest scores on consumer innovativeness also had the highest scores on market mavenism. Are there any students who scored highest on both scales? Does that support the discussion within the chapter about the level of connection between innovators and market mavens?

Table A2.2

Market Mavenism Scale*	Strongly Disagree						Strongly Agree
1. I like introducing new brands and products to my friends.	1	2	3	4	5	6	7
2. I like helping people by providing them with information about many kinds of products.	1	2	3	4	5	6	7
3. People ask me for information about products, places to shop, or sales.	1	2	3	4	5	6	7
4. If someone asked where to get the best buy on several types of products, I could tell him or her where to shop.	1	2	3	4	5	6	7
5. My friends think of me as a good source of information when it comes to new products or sales.	1	2	3	4	5	6	7

* This is the market mavenism scale adopted from Feick, L. F., & Price, L. (1987). The market maven: A diffuser of marketplace information. *Journal of Marketing, 51*(1), 83–97.

Whereas innovators, early adopters, and market mavens may be considered **fashion change agents** because of their impact on the introduction and early stages of acceptance of an innovation, the remaining categories of adopters discussed in this section may be considered **fashion followers** and have not been studied as extensively (Workman & Studak, 2005). **Early majority** consumers adopt innovations before the average consumer. This segment makes up about a third (34%) of all consumers who adopt the innovation. They may spend some time deliberating over adoption of an innovation, certainly longer than the time taken by innovators or early adopters. Early majority consumers may talk about fashion, but they are not usually considered opinion leaders. However, they have an important role in the diffusion process, that of connecting early adopters and another large segment, late majority (Rogers, 2003).

Late majority adopters try an innovation after the average member of the group has. Like early majority adopters, they too account for more than a third of all adopters. They approach an innovation with skepticism and may give in only after experiencing pressure, such as a daughter's relentless effort to convince her mother to buy something other than natural-waist "mom jeans." They tend to have below-average social status, limited financial resources, and very little opinion leadership (Rogers, 2003). Because late majority adopters have limited financial resources, most of their uncertainty regarding an innovation must be removed before the innovation is adopted.

Individuals in the **late adopter** category are the last to adopt an innovation. They make up 16 percent of adopters. Individuals in this category show little to no opinion leadership. Late adopters tend to have lower social status and very limited financial resources, are the oldest of all adopters, and are more isolated, having contact with only family and close friends. They tend to be suspicious of change agents (Rogers, 2003). Because of their limited financial resources and the risk involved in trying innovations, late adopters must be certain that the innovation is successful before they purchase; they tend to be brand loyal (Martinez, Polo, & Flavián, 1998). Firms do not spend a lot to market to late adopters; they let deep discounts do the talking when trying to close out merchandise, such as a 50 percent off sale at the brand's outlet Web site. Fashion followers do not have a high level of need for uniqueness such as is found in fashion change agents (Workman & Kidd, 2000). Therefore, when marketing to fashion followers, fashion firms may want to emphasize being part of a popular trend or the large number of consumers who have successfully adopted the innovation.

This closes the chapter on consumers' role in fashion adoption. It should now be apparent that designers and product developers must work in concert with marketers and merchandisers and use the insights and foster word-of-mouth efforts of consumers to ensure successful diffusion of an innovation.

Chapter Summary

- Individuals move through the five stages of the innovation adoption process for consumer products and fashion trends. The process begins with the awareness stage, followed by the interest stage, the evaluation stage, and the trial stage, and finishes with the adoption stage.
- Individuals may go through the stages of the adoption process at different rates depending on the attributes of the innovation and the characteristics of the individual consumer. Relative advantage, compatibility, complexity, trialability, and observability are attributes of an innovation that affect its rate of adoption.
- A fashion firm may employ various practices to help move consumers through the adoption process, but two consumers exposed to the same practices may move through at different paces because of their personal characteristics including their categorization as innovators, early adopters, early majority adopters, late majority adopters, or late adopters.

Key Terms

- Attributes of the innovation
- Awareness stage
- Compatibility
- Complexity
- Consumer adopter categories
- Early adopters
- Early majority adopters
- Evaluation stage
- Fashion change agents
- Fashion followers
- Innovators
- Late adopters

- Late majority adopters
- Market mavens
- Observability
- Opinion leaders
- Perceived risk
- Product integration
- Product placement
- Relative advantage
- Stages of the adoption process model
- Trial stage
- Trialability

Questions for review and discussion

1. Consider a recent fashion trend that has been around for at least a year. Do you think that you went through each of the five stages (awareness, interest, evaluation, trial, adoption) of the adoption process model in relation to this trend? If you did not go through the adoption stage, are there any factors that may make you reevaluate and try the trend? If so, what are they?

2. Consider a trend or innovation that has caught on quickly (i.e., rapid adoption). How did the five attributes of the innovation affect its rate of adoption? Were all five attributes equally helpful in its rapid acceptance, or were some attributes more important than others?

3. Identify the roles of each adopter category (innovator, early adopter, early majority adopter, late majority adopter, or late adopter). How is each category important in the diffusion of an innovation? How should pricing and advertising strategies change for each of the categories?

Suggested Readings

Gladwell, M. (2002). *The tipping point: How little things can make a big difference*. New York: Little, Brown and Co.

Keller, E., & Berry, J. (2003). *The influentials*. New York: Free Press.

References

Beal, G. M., Rogers, E. M., & Bohlen, J. M. (1957). Validity of the concept of stages in the adoption process. *Rural Sociology, 22*(2), 166–168.

Behling, D. U. (1992). Three and a half decades of fashion adoption research: What have we learned? *Clothing & Textiles Research Journal, 10*(2), 34–41.

Chelminski, P., & Coulter, R. A. (2007). On market mavens and consumer self-confidence: A cross-cultural study. *Psychology & Marketing, 24*(1), 69–91.

Citrin, A. V., Sprott, D. E., Silverman, S. N., & Stem, D. E. (2000). Adoption of Internet shopping: the role of consumer innovativeness. *Industrial Management & Data Systems, 100*(7), 294–300.

Clark, R. A., & Goldsmith, R. E. (2005). Market mavens: Psychological influences. *Psychology & Marketing, 22*(4), 289–312.

DiNardo, A. (2007, March 23). Light bright: Chanel shows off its mastery of makeup lighting. *VMSD*. Retrieved from http://www.vmsd.com/index.php/channel/16/id/11735

Engelland, B. T., Hopkins, C. D., & Larson, D. A. (2001). Market mavenship as an influencer of service quality evaluations. *Journal of Marketing Theory & Practice, 9*(4), 15–26.

Feick, L. F., & Price, L. (1987). The market maven: A diffuser of marketplace information. *Journal of Marketing, 51*(1), 83–97.

Finding profit-driving customer behaviors in big data. *Quantivo*. White paper retrieved from http://www.retailwire.com/Downloads/QuantivoWP_FindingRetailBehaviors.pdf

Fiore, A. M. (2010). *Understanding aesthetics for the merchandising and design professional*. New York: Fairchild.

Gladwell, M. (2002). *The tipping point: How little things can make a big difference*. New York: Little, Brown and Co.

Goldsmith, R. E. (1984). Personality characteristics associated with adaption-innovation. *Journal of Psychology, 117*, 159–165.

Goldsmith, R. E., Flynn, L. R., & Goldsmith, E. B. (2003). Innovative consumers and market mavens. *Journal of Marketing Theory & Practice, 11*(4), 54–65.

Goldsmith, R. E., Freiden, J. B., & Eastman, J. K. (1995). The generality/specificity issue in consumer innovativeness research. *Technovation, 15*(10), 601–611.

Gorchels, L. (2005). *The product manager's handbook*. New York: McGraw-Hill

Hirschman, E. C., & Adcock, W. O. (1978). An examination of innovative communicators, opinion leaders and innovators for men's fashion apparel. *Advances in Consumer Research, 5*, 308–313.

Holak, S. L., & Lehmann, D. R. (1990). Intention and the dimensions of innovation: An exploratory model. *Journal of Product Innovation Management, 7*, 59–73.

Im, S., Bayus, B. L., & Mason, C. H. (2003). An empirical study of innate consumer innovativeness, personal characteristics, and new-product adoption behavior. *Journal of the Academy of Marketing Science, 31*(1), 61–73.

Im, S., Mason, C. H., & Houston, M. B. (2007). Does innate consumer innovativeness relate to new product/service adoption behavior? The intervening role of social learning via vicarious innovativeness. *Journal of the Academy of Marketing Science, 35,* 63–75.

Joez Jeans posts excellent Q4, positive for 2010. (2010, February 4). *World Market Media.* Retrieved from http://www.worldmarketmedia.com/779/section.aspx/852/post/joez-joez-jeans-posts-excellent-q4-positive-for-2010

Kim, H-J., Fiore, A. M., Niehm, L., & Jeong, M. (2010). Creative class consumers' behavioral intentions towards pop-up retail. *International Journal of Retailing and Distribution Management, 38*(2), 133–154.

Martinez, E., Polo, Y., & Flavián, C. (1998). The acceptance and diffusion of new consumer durables: Differences between first and last adopters. *Journal of Marketing, 15*(4), 323–342.

Midgley, F. D., & Dowling, G. R. (1978). Innovativeness: The concept and its measurement. *Journal of Consumer Research, 4*(March), 323–342.

Miller, J. (2010, May 15). ISU grad is "florist to the stars." *DesMoinesRegister.com.* Retrieved from http://www.desmoinesregister.com/apps/pbcs.dll/article?AID=20105150301

Nanotechnology and textiles. (n.d.). *Strategic applications integrating nano science.* Retrieved from http://www.sainsce.com/textiles.aspx

Nussbaum, E. (2008, October 5). What Tina Fey would do for a SoyJoy. *New York.* Retrieved from http://nymag.com/news/features/51014/

Painter, J. J., & Pinegar, M. L. (1971). Post high teens and fashion innovation. *Journal of Marketing Research, 8,* 368–369.

Phau, I., & Lo, C-C. (2004). Profiling fashion innovators: A study of self-concept, impulse buying and Internet purchase intent. *Journal of Fashion Marketing and Management, 8*(4), 399–411.

Pilkington, E. (2008, July 22). Product placement advertising makes its way into U.S. news programmes. *Guardian.co.uk.* Retrieved from http://www.guardian.co.uk/world/2008/jul/22/usa.mediabusiness

Reynolds, F. D., & Darden, W. R. (1973). Fashion theory and pragmatics: The case of the midi. *Journal of Retailing, 49,* 51–62.

Rogers, E. M. (2003). *Diffusion of innovations.* New York: Free Press.

Ruvio, A., & Shoham, A. (2007). Innovativeness, exploratory behavior, market mavenship, and opinion leadership: An empirical examination in the Asian context. *Psychology & Marketing, 24*(8), 703–722.

Schrank, H., Sugawara, A., & Kim, M. (1982). Comparison of Korean and American fashion leaders. *Home Economics Research Journal, 10,* 227–234.

Slama, M. E., & Williams, T. G. (1990). Generalization of the market maven's information provision tendency across product categories. *Advances in Consumer Research, 17,* 48–52.

Sproles, G. B. (1981). Analyzing fashion life cycles—principles and perspectives. *Journal of Marketing, 45*(Fall), 116–124.

Steenkamp, J-B., ter Hofstede, F., & Wedel, M. (1999). A cross-national investigation into the individual and national cultural antecedents of consumer innovativeness. *Journal of Marketing, 63*(April), 55–69.

Toffler, B., & Imber, J. (2000). *Dictionary of marketing terms.* New York: Barron's Educational Series. Retrieved from http://www.allbusiness.com/glossaries/perceived-risk/4963320–1.html

Wangenheim, F. V. (2005). Postswitching negative word of mouth. *Journal of Service Research, 8*(1), 67–78.

Wiedmann, K. P., Walsh, G., & Mitchell, V. W. (2001). The German manmaven: An agent for diffusing market information. *Journal of Marketing Communications, 7*(4), 195–212.

Workman, J. E., & Kidd, L. K. (2000). Use of the need for uniqueness scale to characterize fashion consumer groups. *Clothing & Textiles Research Journal, 18*(4), 227–236.

Workman, J. E., & Studak, C. M. (2005). Relationships among fashion consumers, locus of control, boredom proneness, boredom coping and intrinsic enjoyment. *International Journal of Consumer Studies, 31*(1), 66–75.

Yoh, E. (2005). Adoption of fragranced textile products by segmented markets: Application of the innovation adoption theory. *Journal of the Textile Institute, 96*(3), 157–167.

3

THE PROCESS AND METHODS OF FASHION TREND ANALYSIS AND FORECASTING

Objectives

- Understand the process of fashion trend analysis and forecasting
- Understand how sociocultural factors influence trends in the fashion industry
- Understand the role and methods of short-term fashion forecasting, including color, textiles, and style forecasting
- Understand the role and methods of long-term fashion forecasting

The process of fashion trend analysis and forecasting

The fashion system is a dialogue between professionals in the fashion industry, who propose innovations, and consumers, who selectively adopt the created innovations. In the previous chapter, consumers' roles in fashion adoption were discussed, along with various product and consumer attributes that affect acceptance and rate of adoption of new fashion products. In this chapter, the process and the methods of fashion trend analysis and forecasting as a starting point for product development are discussed. The process of fashion trend analysis and forecasting is represented by a new model with three components: environment, product, and market.

Trend analysis and forecasting as the beginning stage in the product development process

Forecasting new trends in fashion is complex and difficult, because fashion is constantly changing and because it is affected by numerous factors. Professionals in the textile and apparel industry begin predicting trends about two years before a particular style is marketed. Clarifying where trend analysis and forecasting are positioned in the product development process before moving on to a discussion of the process of fashion trend analysis and forecasting will give readers an idea of its role in product development.

Facing shorter fashion cycles, increasingly sophisticated consumers, and heavy retail competition, traditional retail buyers have a role in creating products at the retail level; they exert their influence through their product development divisions (Gaskill, 1992). A retail **product development** division is responsible for the conceptualization, planning, development, and presentation of product lines (Gaskill, 1992); it tries to better understand its target market in order to interpret and propose the trends for a season on the basis of projected consumer preferences (Johne & Snelson, 1990; Sproles, 1979).

Wickett, Gaskill, and Damhorst (1999) tested the validity of Gaskill's (1992) Product Development Model and modified the stages in the original model based on new data. As shown in Figure 3.1, nine activities are incorporated into the model. The preliminary stage of product development begins with an in-depth "**trend analysis**," labeled "inspirational search of trends," which was added by Wickett et al. to the revised model. During this stage, ideas for products are collected from a variety of sources. As part of their in-depth search for sources of inspiration, planners give careful consideration to seasonal predictions related to color, fabrication, surface design, silhouette, style, and the overall direction of fashion. Once trends are researched, the collected items, such as photographs, magazine clippings, and fabric samples, are brought together for further analysis. Keeping in mind criteria such as the company's image, its target customer, and its strategic plans, planners develop seasonal themes or concepts in the "theme development" stage. Next, the physical characteristics of the seasonal line are developed to reinforce the seasonal theme. "Palette development" determines both base and accent groups of colors; then, the "structural fabric decisions" concerning fiber content and fabric structure and "fabric surface design directions" follow. In the next stage, "silhouette and style directions," silhouettes and styles are decided. After the seasonal line is visualized, "prototype pattern making, construction, and analysis" activity takes place to develop samples of the proposed line. This is followed by "line presentation." During line presentation, the proposed seasonal line is narrowed down for final "line adoption" into the company's offering. Throughout the development process, all internal factors, such as the merchandising process and the defined target market, and external factors, such as foreign and domestic markets, impact the development process (Wickett et al., 1999).

A model of the fashion trend analysis and forecasting process

As noted earlier, the **fashion forecasting process** begins about two years in advance of the retailing season for new products. Broadly, this process encompasses the three components of environment, market, and product (see Figure 3.2). First, the **environment** is scanned to search for current and near-future trends in the economic, political, social, and cultural (e.g., art, music, fashion) arenas (sectors). An understanding of the long-term direction of the society can also be helpful. The information is then analyzed, interpreted, and synthesized. Professionals who are involved in forecasting always observe what is happening both instinctively and consciously.

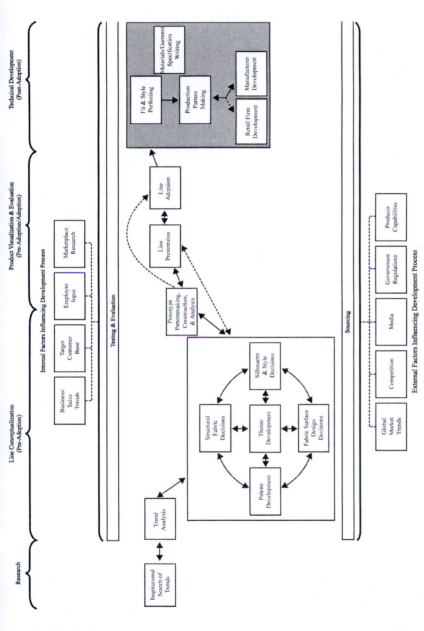

Solid lines denote the progression of apparel products through the development process.
Broken lines denote alternative development routes that may be taken.
■ Denotes stages that may not be performed in-house by the retail organization.

Figure 3.1 Trend analysis and forecasting as a starting point in the product development process: Wicket, Gaskill, and Damhorst's model (1999).

Source: Wickett, J. L., Gaskill, L. R., & Damhorst, M. L. (1999). Apparel retail product development: Model testing and expansion. *Clothing & Textiles Research Journal, 17*(1), 22.

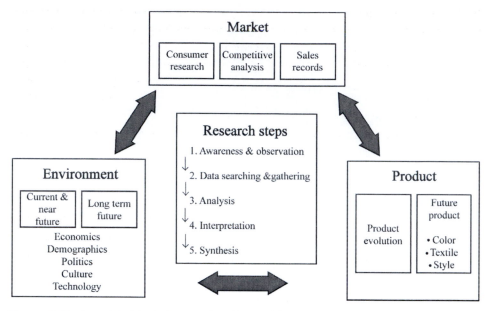

Figure 3.2 A model of the fashion trend analysis and forecasting process.
Source: Developed by Eundeok Kim.

Market research that focuses on consumers, competing companies, and sales records is conducted. As forecasts can vary depending on the characteristics of the target market, it is important to research and understand consumer demographics, lifestyles, values, attitudes, and behaviors. In recent years, consumer segments have diversified into many separate market niches. Different forecasts for individual lines should therefore be developed for specific segments. The activities of competing companies that operate in similar product categories and that compete for similar consumer segments should also be monitored. Over time, this comparison allows for the benchmarking of activities and the development of an accurate view of the market environment. In addition, previous sales records should be analyzed to establish sales trends within the firm. Rising sales statistics implies that the styles are increasingly being adopted; declining sales show that the styles have passed their peak on the consumption curve.

At the stage of forecasting new products for the upcoming season, the evolution of products within a category or across categories is analyzed first to predict the next trends. Then, color, textile, and style trends are researched via various sources, such as **trade shows** and publications, fashion magazines, and street fashions. Services that monitor trends are another important source of information. Color palettes should be decided about two years ahead of a retailing season, which is the basis for textile manufacturers' fiber and fabric production and surface design.

Textile forecasting begins about eighteen months in advance of a retailing season, and style forecasting begins about one year in advance. However, given the current, increasingly short fashion cycle, a shorter forecasting cycle is becoming necessary.

The elements of the trend analysis and forecasting process—environment, market, and product—in the apparel industry are illustrated in Figure 3.2. For each element, **awareness and observation**, **data searching and information gathering**, **analysis**, **interpretation**, and **synthesis** are the different phases of the research process. The multidirectional arrows that link the three elements represent their interconnection.

The methods of fashion trend analysis and forecasting

Forecasting is both an art and a science (Sproles & Burns, 1994). It is an art because forecasts are often based on intuition, good judgment, and creativity. It is also a science because forecasters use analytical concepts and models to predict forthcoming trends in systematic ways (Sproles & Burns, 1994).

Technological innovations such as the Internet and fast fashion have accelerated the rate of fashion change. In 1998, the life span of a fashion trend was approximately one year, while in 2003 it was only a few months or even a few weeks (Keiser & Garner, 2003). Presently, it has become even shorter—every week or every other week new styles are adopted. The accelerated rates of fashion change make forecasting trends more difficult.

Two types of fashion forecasting are used: **short-term forecasting**, which predicts trends one to two years in the future and focuses on new products, especially color, textile, and style, and **long-term forecasting**, which predicts trends five or more years in the future and focuses on the directions of the fashion industry, particularly in materials, design, production, and retailing. Long-term forecasts contribute to a fashion firm's development strategies and help it make decisions related to repositioning or extending product lines, initiating new businesses, and reviving brand images.

The sociocultural context

Fashion forecasters first scan the environment to recognize sociocultural trends. Both the current spirit of the times (i.e., the zeitgeist) and long-term forecasts, or megatrends, are researched.

Zeitgeist: The spirit of the time

All cultural components reflect the spirit of the times; thus, the **sociocultural context** or **zeitgeist** must be considered in forecasting new fashion products for the future. Various forces in a consumer's environment can affect future consumer demand for fashions. Therefore, as noted in chapter 1, an understanding of broad trends in society, including the changing state of the economy, demographic trends, politics, the changing cultural environment, and technological developments, is important (Sproles & Burns, 1994). In addition to the spirit of the time, variations in different national contexts should be considered. Uncovering the nature of the social context requires observation, information gathering, analysis, interpretation, and synthesis. The sources for researching the social context are numerous; electronic communications and media are a few examples. A forecaster must become like a sponge, soaking up every aspect of the social context, including current issues or events in the government and economy, demographics, world and national news, sports and entertainment, the arts, science and technology, health, religion, and lifestyle (Fiore & Kimle, 1997), as illustrated in Figure 3.3.

A changing economy has a fundamental influence on consumer demand. Factors such as the rate of inflation and consumers' personal incomes determine consumers' buying power. Domestic and global economic conditions have a major impact on consumers' confidence in their financial future, and this is also reflected

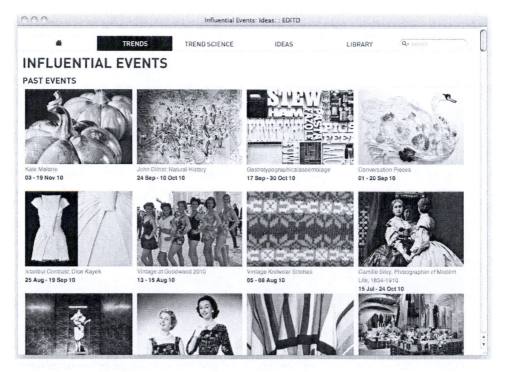

Figure 3.3 Sociocultural factors influencing fashion trends.
Source: EDITD. Retrieved from http://editd.com/features/#ideas.

in consumers' choices. For example, when the economy is doing well, fashion may be extravagant; when it is doing poorly, consumers are conservative in their preferences and tend to prefer classic or functional styles (Keiser & Garner, 2003). In the recession that began in 2008, sales in the U.S. luxury fashion segment dropped 27.6 percent between December 2007 and December 2008, according to statistics supplied in a MasterCard report. Consumers have turned toward designer affinity lines created for recession-chic stores such as H&M and Target, as well as toward classic fashion pieces that will last. As trepidation over the economy has affected personal budgets and weighed on the minds of consumers, the timeless ethos of the preppy style has taken hold of the retail apparel sector, as evidenced by strong numbers recently posted by clothing brands traditionally associated with classic or preppy styles (Szustek, 2009).

Demographic trends such as changes in the population can also affect trends in fashion. For example, the growing population of older consumers is an increasingly important segment of the fashion market (Sproles & Burns, 1994), so an increasing number of advertisers and marketers use older models and spokespersons (Moschis, Lee, Mathur, & Strautman, 2000). Today, the familiar faces of older models frequently appear in commercials, and a growing number of spokespersons are in their fifties, sixties, and even seventies. Today, older models frequently appear in commercials, and a growing number of spokespersons and hosts are in their fifties, sixties, and even seventies. For example, popular talk-show host Lawrence Harvey, known publicly as "Larry King," the host of Larry King Live on CNN, has only recently retired in his late seventies. The "aging" trend is a global phenomenon; in China, the number of people age sixty-five and over is expected to triple in just thirty years, while, in the United States, it is estimated that the number of people in this age bracket has doubled. Mature Americans, especially women, are as fashionable nowadays as their younger counterparts. Those with the highest levels of income and education are the most fashion conscious. Understanding generational differences is important to marketing fashion items effectively to different generations. A company that understands these differences will be able to create products that better speak to different generations and to advertise and market to those generations effectively.

Current events in politics and world news also have a major impact on fashion. Politics often reflects the mores and expectations of a society (Keiser & Garner, 2003). For example, the opening of trade relations with China inspired some designers to adopt traditional Chinese silhouettes and design elements (Keiser & Garner, 2003). Furthermore, the recent fashion for camouflage prints and military wear reflects the current climate of war. In his February 2009 collection for New York Fashion Week, Marcus Wainwright of Rag & Bone released a mini-parade of military greatcoats, camouflage anoraks, and variations on the field jacket, with its multiple pockets and gusseted cuffs. Military influences were already widespread before the latest shows. For much of 2009, interpretations of battle gear infiltrated the style world, "tracing a jagged trajectory up from the campus and the concert stadium and onto the runways of Balmain, Marc Jacobs, and Burberry then back again into mainstream shops" such as those of DKNY and Gap with stylized versions of the field jacket (Ferla, 2010). This is hardly surprising after nearly a decade of Americans fighting in Iraq and Afghanistan (Ferla, 2010).

Changes in consumer lifestyles, cultural values, trends in the arts, and pop culture can also be powerful influences on future fashions. For example, individualism and personal freedom have relaxed the norms of society and expanded the range of styles adopted. At the same time, the interest in sustainability has popularized organic cotton, the color green, and subtle colors from natural dyes—all a manifestation of the recent focus on protecting the environment (Fiore & Kimle, 1997). In alignment with this global focus, antifur organizations have rallied against the use of animal products in fashion, so designers and retailers now emphasize the use of faux fur.

Cultural diversity has also affected fashion by introducing and popularizing various ethnic styles. For instance, Asian movies invaded Hollywood in the early 1990s, which inspired a preference for Asian designs in fashion (Sproles & Burns, 1994). Like cultural diversity, the arts have had a major impact on fashion. Designers and fashion forecasters pay attention to major art exhibitions and historic costume exhibitions. For instance, an exhibit of paintings by Monet, van Gogh, or Matisse can influence seasonal color palettes and textile patterns. The exhibit, at the Metropolitan Museum of Art in New York in 2001, of clothes worn by Jacqueline Kennedy spurred an interest in the ladylike ensemble dressing of the 1960s (Keiser & Garner, 2003). Examining the fashion context is also important. For instance, with the emergence of fast-fashion chains, consumers have begun to buy clothes closer to the season for which they are intended, forcing companies to shorten the product development cycle (Frings, 2008).

Technological innovation and development can affect consumer demand for fashion items. The ubiquity of the Internet and the globalization of fashion have enabled apparel firms to produce immediate designer knockoffs, so the trend cycle has been accelerated. Once a style hits the runway, it often quickly saturates stores at all price points. The biggest task for retailers is to figure out which styles will become fashion basics and which styles will be fads (Sproles & Burns, 1994). There are almost continuous innovations and technological developments in the production of textiles and clothing; recent innovations have included new fiber technology, new finishes for fabrics, wearable apparel with enhanced functions, mass customization, body-scanning technology, and digital textile printing. Now you have a better understanding of how the spirit of the times influences new fashion products for the future and that it must be considered in forecasting. Case 3.1 illustrates a forecasting firm's practices in the fashion industry. Try Activity 3.1, which will give you an opportunity to practice forecasting a fashion trend based on the spirit of the time.

CASE 3.1. FORECASTING FASHION IN SOUTH KOREA: FIRST VIEW KOREA—PFIN

PFIN is the brand name of First View Korea, a partner of First View in the United States. CEO Chungmin Lee launched First View in September 2000. First View Korea provides two types of services: consulting and information. The consulting service includes branding and planning. For branding, they develop strategies to support a brand. For planning, they create or contribute to designing and make suggestions for exhibitions or material developments. Following is the author's interview with Chungmin Lee in July 2009.

EK: Could you tell me what services you offer in detail?
CL: PFIN forecasts megatrends and design trends. We analyze the global market to help trading companies who want to do business in the global market. When we launched First View Korea in 2000, our business was the first information service completely based online at that time. While watching the online publications on the First View site in 1999, we envisioned that fashion trends would change faster. So we thought we would do the collection seminar the earliest in Korea with the information from the First View site.

In 2000, when we launched, we held a seminar, presenting our analysis of the collections from Paris only in one week after the Paris collections. Since that time, our collection seminars have become our major product. We attract about 2,000 professionals for the women's collection seminar and anywhere from 1,000 to 1,500 for our men's collection seminar. What we began in 2000 was very innovative at the time because prior to our web publication, fashion publications were only accessible two months after the collections were debuted through fashion magazine reports. At the time, magazine sales were negatively affected by us.

EK: How do you analyze collections?
CL: We receive photos of a season's fashion collections, then we analyze trends based on the photos. We develop forecasts for mood, color story, items, details, and how products should be made for the next season. Korean companies plan for the next twenty-six weeks whereas the United States has a fifty-two-week planning system, so currently, most Korean companies are planning for [spring/summer] 2010 while most U.S. firms have already prepared for the summer and are beginning to prepare for [fall/winter] 2010. In the United States, trend services provide big pictures or directions as opposed to specific styles. When we began, we suggested specific styles that we thought would become fashion and Korean firms became accustomed to it.

When we look at the collection analyses performed by U.S. style sites such as Trend Stop and Worth Global Style Network (WGSN), we are not convinced by their forecasts because the lifestyles of the United States, Europe, and Korea are different. For example, formal dress (evening wear) is very important to U.S. fashion but not to Asian fashion. Some of the information is useful to the Korean market, but some is not applicable to it. The reason we decided to do trend services was that we thought the Asian market needed particular attention because it was distinct and unique and would grow larger than the

U.S. or European markets. We thought that trends could be created in the Asian market, and searching trends from the point of the Asian market was needed. Trend information circulation used to begin in the United States and Europe because they had better access to information, but, now, we have extensive information collected even faster than big trend firms such as Nelly Rodi. We have monitors [trend spotters] in seven fashion cities—New York, Los Angeles, Milan, Paris, Tokyo, Shanghai, and Beijing—so, we are able to conduct in-depth research in specific countries and collect detailed, relevant information. . . . Thanks to the Internet, I could do this type of online business in Korea. But now, ironically, due to the Internet, brands or consumers have faster access to information, and they knew what has been created better than we do.

EK: *What do you think the role of forecasting is?*

CL: It is to provide assurance to the uncertainty of the future. Usually, clients who use our service have some ideas about the future, so the role of forecasting makes clients more confident about their ideas. We speak not only to our clients but also to the media about what is in fashion. The media directs consumers to purchase the styles.

EK: *I assume your trend forecasts have not always been correct. When your forecasts were not right, what did you do to improve them for the next time?*

CL: I think that the most important element of trend forecasting is timing. For instance, we predicted that the "Ruby Look" (forty-five-plus women who dress like "a princess") would be important in July of 2007. However, it was not a trend in 2007; instead, in 2008, the Ruby Look became a trend. Although it eventually became popular, our forecast was not successful for the fashion businesses. Our timing has been off, but I do not recall a time when we were completely incorrect about a trend. One time, we thought that jackets would be very popular, and there were many people who were wearing jackets in the street, but sales were not increasing. We had forecasted that jackets would be in fashion, so apparel companies made many jackets, but they did not sell. Here, our forecasts were correct in terms of fashion; even though that happened—our forecasts were not wrong in terms of fashion, but businesses did not profit. So we learned that we had to be careful not to be very specific.

EK: *Do Korean firms want you to predict very specific styles?*

CL: Yes, for instance, once they wanted us to forecast the length of jacket—whether it would be below the hip or mid-thigh. We had met their expectation to be specific, but we thought . . . trends and what businesses produce should be diverse and that such specificity was not desirable. We usually have 1,000 to 2,000 audience members at our seminars and if we say this and that are important, then all companies make those and all the products became similar, and if we forecast that a particular style will become important, all of the companies will produce that style, and all of the products began to be too similar. Instead, we thought that we should provide more general direction. . . . In the future, planning will be more helpful for the forecasting business. Forecasting companies who do R&D or provide marketing or execution will make money rather than, like in the past, companies who predict trends only. Now, unlike the past, many apparel companies have trend analysts in their firms, so providing more general megatrends will still be profitable. Additionally, there is no trend that fits all companies. Some trends can be the right answer for some people while the trend can be the wrong answer for others.

We usually identify four trends at the seminar. It is very important not to predict incorrect trends. We cannot identify all trends, anyway. And the evaluation on which is right and wrong trend is subjective. Of course, that depends on whether the trends are adopted or not, but the trend is market specific. Some trends are suitable in some markets, but some are not in other markets.

EK: What are the differences between Korea and the United States related to forecasting? Cultural values and preferences?

CL: Yes, and also, materials are different. Tastes are different between Koreans, Europeans, and Americans. Feelings are different; skin color is different. For example, Korean women tend to like body-conforming clothing, not fluid clothing, although that seems to be changing now. . . . I am surprised that foreign companies do not know more about differences in the Korean consumer. They think Koreans have the same buying behaviors as Westerners, but there are many cultural differences, like the fact that Koreans wear jeans in different ways than Americans do.

Source

Interview with Chungmin Lee, CEO of First View Korea—PFIN, by Eundeok Kim, Seoul, South Korea, July 2, 2009.

ACTIVITY 3.1. FORECASTING A FASHION TREND ON THE BASIS OF THE SPIRIT OF THE TIME (ZEITGEIST)

When beginning forecasting for the next season, a fashion forecaster first scans the environment because the spirit of the time is one of the major influences on fashion. Read and bring to class five articles on any aspects of the current society, including economics, demographics, politics, culture, and technology. You can find the articles in various sources such as online news services, newspapers, and magazines. Identify the current sociocultural trend that the article suggests and label it; then forecast a fashion trend for men, women, or children for the next season that reflects the social trend. Create five styles, with detailed descriptions of the design. Explain the relationship between the current sociocultural trend and the predicted fashion trend, using the design factors of color, textile, and style. You should be specific about the target market's demographic and psychographic factors.

Megatrends: Long-term forecast

As discussed earlier, long-term forecasting seeks to identify trends that are five years or more out. Long-term forecasts help companies to evaluate current business practices; reposition a product or reconsider how it relates to customers; formulate a strategic plan; and understand and evaluate short-term forecasting. Forecasters consider many factors: shifts in demographics that can restructure society; changes in industry and market structure; differences in consumer interests, values, and motivation; breakthroughs in technology and science; changes in the economic picture; and alterations in political, cultural, and economic alliances between countries (Brannon, 2005). Most trend spotters are more receptive to change and make connections using imaginative thinking. **Trend spotting** must be carried out continuously and systematically to be effective. A number of marketing consultants specialize in long-term trend forecasting; these companies alert the industry to shifting sociocultural trends that will affect what the consumer wants (Keiser & Garner, 2003). For instance, the rapid impact of technology is a long-term trend that has contributed to a shift toward business-casual dress over the past decade. This trend has accelerated as more business is conducted via the Internet and the telephone and there is less face-to-face interaction during the business day (Keiser & Garner, 2003).

There are several methods that long-term forecasters often employ: content analysis, interviewing, observation, and scenario writing. The methods are discussed in detail in chapter 4. One of the most common methods is **content analysis** of media sources. **John Naisbitt**, a futurist and consultant, published *Megatrends* in 1982. He coined the term "**megatrend**" to refer to major shifts in society that have a definite impact on individual lifestyles. His method for research focused on scanning a variety of media sources for both editorial and advertising content to identify patterns, which he would then analyze to determine what those patterns reveal. In the book, Naisbitt identified ten megatrends, including a move toward an information-based economy, the dual compensations of high-tech and high-touch products (high-touch products have soft contours and cozy, handmade, or artsy attributes), and the shift to a global economy (Brannon, 2005). His most recent book, *High Tech High Touch: Technology and Our Search for Meaning* (1999), hypothesizes how technology will influence our culture as the new millennium progresses and suggests that the challenge will be to embrace technology that preserves our humanness and to reject technology that intrudes upon it (Brannon, 2005).

Faith Popcorn cofounded the company Brain Reserve in 1974 and is known for her books *The Popcorn Report* (1991), *Clicking* (1997), and *Evolution* (2000). Popcorn is a popular speaker about the future and works with various clients in her marketing consultancy. Her forecasting methodology involves scanning a continuous stream of periodicals, monitoring pop culture, shopping stores across the country and abroad, and interviewing consumers about a variety of product categories (Brannon, 2005). Popcorn (1991) argued that trends are predictive because they start small and gradually gather momentum. She observed,

> If you can connect the dots between the inception of a trend and the impact it will have on your business, then you can fine-tune your product to fit the trend. And because trends [lifestyle trends, not style trends] take on average ten years to work through the culture and reach all market levels, the momentum of the current trends will propel your business, ahead of the end of the decade or beyond.

Each of these trends contains enough energy, enough variety, enough stability, to keep working its way through the market arena. To make your product or business on-trend, you will need to understand how the trends work together to define the future. (p. 67)

She also mentions that the best way to pick up on early indications of new trends is to understand the evolution of current trends. According to Popcorn, trends go through different chartable stages, and, by the time a trend phases itself out, it will have gone through many transformations. In closing this section, complete Activity 3.2, which will give you a chance to explore long-term forecasting—the future trends in the textile and apparel industry.

ACTIVITY 3.2. LONG-TERM FORECASTING: THE TRENDS IN THE TEXTILE AND APPAREL INDUSTRY IN THE NEXT FIVE TO TEN YEARS

Imagine the changes in the U.S. society and in the world in the next five to ten years. How will the trends influence the textiles and apparel industry with regard to materials, design, production, and retailing? Write a scenario that describes a situation or experience.

Forecasting new products

In this section, we discuss short-term forecasting as it relates to products. The analysis of **product evolution**, which helps to identify future trends, is followed by a discussion of ways to forecast future products in terms of color, textile, and style. A discussion of market research including consumer research, competitive analysis, and sales analysis is presented in the following chapter.

Recognizing patterns of a product

What consumers are going to purchase next year is a central question on the minds of many fashion professionals. As new fashions evolve from previously established fashions, recognizing the transition of a product over time can help predict the future direction of the fashion products (Fiore & Kimle, 1997). Analyzing the evolution of products can be conducted across product categories or within a category. When analyzing across time, fashion professionals analyze a sampling of products from consecutive years. For instance, an examination of the change in skirt length of women's wear or of the shoulder shape of men's suits can help forecast the product's evolution in the next season. Analysts can then identify trends within particular product categories (Fiore & Kimle, 1997).

THE PROCESS AND METHODS

By analyzing the rate of acceptance and the current level of acceptance, analysts can estimate how much longer the trend may extend. For instance, the diffusion curve may indicate whether the style is growing, reaching market saturation, or beginning its decline. A forecast can then be made on the basis of the current extent of diffusion, as indicated by the curve and the amount of consumer demand remaining. Although the diffusion curve is a basic reference for determining the future strength and duration of a trend, some additional questions can make the forecast even more precise; such questions may turn on whether the style will be a fad, a fashion, or a classic or whether the adopters of a style will repeat the purchase (Sproles & Burns, 1994). As discussed, recognizing patterns of a product in previous years is an important step in forecasting new products. Try Activity 3.3, which will help you better understand how to analyze the evolution of an apparel item.

ACTIVITY 3.3. ANALYZING THE EVOLUTION OF MEN'S JACKETS IN THE PAST TEN YEARS

Choose a men's fashion magazine or fashion show photos posted online. Bring at least ten examples of photos of men's jackets to class (one from each year). Collect the photos systematically. For example, you could choose photos from the same month of the year over ten years. Compare the lengths, widths, and details (e.g., lapel and pockets) to determine stylistic changes during the time period. The descriptions should be accompanied by a chart with years on the top row and items for analysis in the left column. Identify patterns of change, and predict the styles for the next year.

Color

Color is a powerful tool in positioning apparel products in the marketplace. Color has been identified as the design factor that most influences a consumer when he or she is making a purchasing decision (Eckman, Damhorst, & Kadolph, 1990). Brand image is also highly defined in terms of color. A brand image must be cohesive and must evolve seasonally without changing so much that it risks losing its customer base. Consumers frequently demonstrate loyalty to those brands that offer colors that they feel suit them (Linton, 1994).

Color also evokes symbolic associations, so marketers carefully use the psychological power of colors to communicate with consumers (Brannon, 2005). The association between color and emotion has been studied by numerous researchers. According to Frances, in her article "Color Facts and Color Effects," red is associated with passion, strength, and love, whereas yellow is associated with happiness and creativity. Blue is related to trust, loyalty, and truth, whereas green means growth, abundance, renewal, and hope. Orange is associated with energy, contentment, and sensuality, while white means perfection, harmony, and sincerity. Black signifies formality, dignity, authority, and glamour (cited in Lamkins, 2010). Although marketing may influence a consumer's purchase decision, ultimately a consumer's choice of color is based upon personal preference (Diane & Cassidy, 2005). In general, younger generations are most open to wearing any color that is trendy, whereas older customers tend to limit their choice of colors to those that they believe look good on them. Thus, color forecasts need to be interpreted for specific consumer groups and market categories (Keiser & Garner, 2003). Using consumer color preference correctly improves sales.

Besides personal preferences, cultural differences in color preference also affect consumer choice. For instance, European colors have to be modified for the American market because, generally, Americans like their colors cleaner, brighter, and less complex, whereas European colors tend to be darker, deeper, and more neutral (Linton, 1994). The symbolic meaning of color in different cultures is also important, as the connotation of color varies across cultures. For instance, black is a mourning color in most Western cultures, whereas white is the funeral color in some Eastern countries, such as China and Korea. Violet is the funeral color in Turkey, and yellow in Burma (Lauer & Pentak, 2008).

Some researchers have argued that color cycles run in predictable sequences. They have found evidence of swings from high-chroma (bright) colors to multi-colors to subdued colors to earth tones to aromatics to purple phases and back to high-chroma colors. As long as a seven-year period has been identified as the lapse between a preference for cool colors and one for warm tones. Cycles can be based on hue, intensity, and color temperature (Diane & Cassidy, 2005).

Color trends are usually directly linked with the state of the world. For instance, when environmental issues, global unrest, political strife, economic instability, and wars are present, consumers seek security from the Earth and tend to go back to nature and to time-honored reminiscences (Lamkins, 2010). In times of uncertainty, consumers are most comfortable with colors that are a reminder of familiar things. Color subliminally evokes emotional responses in our psyche, and trends in color reflect a balance of these unconscious emotional responses to color and the stable assurances that the Earth promises in natural hues, tints, and shades. By grounding ourselves in familiar and safe surroundings, we comfort our innermost selves (Lamkins, 2010).

In developing a new collection of apparel products, the first step is to select a color palette. Color forecasting is conducted about two years in advance of the retailing season for new products. The decision about a seasonal color palette is the basis for dyeing yarns and for designing fabric for all the styles in the line (Diane & Cassidy, 2005). Textile firms must have forecasted trends eighteen months in advance; designers and merchandisers need them one year in advance. Forecasters and designers sort and gather information from a variety of sources before making color decisions (Keiser & Garner, 2003). They attend trade shows and fashion shows held in major fashion cities, such as Paris, Milan, London, and New York. Premiere Vision is recognized as one of the most popular and important exhibitions at which fabric manufacturers exhibit their current and new fabric ranges as a source of inspiration. The three-day show acts as a color filter for the fashion industry, largely because of the availability of the exhibition's color card, which ensures that the exhibition relates to the color stories set by the panel for that season, instilling and promoting a consensual theme (Diane & Cassidy, 2005).

Top designers present their new collections twice each year in runway shows held in the major fashion cities. Retail buyers, fashion editors, and designers from all over the world attend these shows and analyze the collections, which can influence the seasonal fashion direction (Frings, 2008). A trend may appear in a new or unique fabrication, color, silhouette, or other design elements that appear in multiple collections. Fashion professionals also visit showrooms of designers and shop and watch fashion in major fashion cities (Frings, 2008) and monitor street fashions that originate with consumers in these cities (Sproles & Burns, 1994). They also subscribe to trade publications, magazines, newspapers, and online newsletters.

Trend forecasting companies also help the fashion businesses understand general color trends and provide palettes of new colors that they predict will be popular. They provide fashion reporting, forecasting, and consulting on a subscription basis and publish trend forecasts that include descriptions, sketches, fabric swatches, and color samples for garments for the next season (Frings, 2008). Figure 3.4 shows examples of color forecasts, and Figure 3.5 shows a textiles forecast for fall/winter 2011 created by PFIN, a forecasting firm in South Korea. Some forecasting companies specialize in color forecasting. The Color Marketing Group and The Color Association of the United States are the largest color marketing associations in the world. Members of these groups are color specialists who represent some of the biggest companies in the world (Keiser & Garner, 2003). Other sources include Pantone Color Institute, Color Portfolio, Cotton Inc., International Color Authority, and Fashion Forecasting Services. Everyone at the color meetings (e.g., fiber manufacturers, designers, and forecasters) brings his own color storyboard. Then, after discussions, a color palette of between thirty-five and fifty colors is agreed upon. The forecasters identify stable classic colors, fashion-driven colors, and new directional colors for their specific target markets (Hope & Walch, 1990).

Color systems are another type of color resource. Companies like Pantone keep a permanent library of dyed colors in color families. They distribute color cards to their customers, who use the samples as standards for choosing colors for merchandise and dyeing fabrics. Color forecasting specialists such as Doneger Creative Services and The Color Box offer subscription color services for a fee. These services generally release their forecasts eighteen months prior to a season. This is about six months after organizations such as The Color Marketing Group and The Color Association of the United States have made their color forecasts and broken them down into predictions for various markets and price points (Frings, 2008).

Fashion is a reflection of our times and of the prevailing ideas in our society. Fashion concepts spread across a wide range of products via fashion components such as

Figure 3.4 Color stories by PFIN.
Source: PFIN.

Figure 3.5 A textiles forecast.
Source: PFIN.

apparel, accessories, furnishings, architecture, interior, automobiles, and electronics (Keiser & Garner, 2003). However, color cycles are different in different industries. Color cycles in the apparel industry occur approximately every two years, whereas, in interior design, the color period is considerably longer—from seven to twelve years (Linton, 1994). In recent years, the time lag in popularity across different types of products has grown shorter; for example, when red apparel was being featured a few years ago, the same color was observed by trend spotters in French tableware, Italian accessories, and U.S. kitchen appliances (Brannon, 2005).

Textiles

Fiber producers and mills start projecting **textile** trends eighteen months ahead of the retailing season. The task of researching seasonal fabrics goes on at the same time as color research and the color story are being planned. Many services that provide color forecasts also offer fabric forecasts. These sources alert a product developer to new technology, fibers, blends, and finishes by providing descriptions, swatches, and sketches of possible applications (Keiser & Garner, 2003). Fashion professionals rely on these sources and on fabric and yarn shows to keep up to date. Numerous domestic and international fabric and yarn shows are held each year to give product developers an overview of what is available (Keiser & Garner, 2003). Premiere Vision in Paris is probably the biggest fabric show in the world. Other shows include European Textile Select Show, Expofil, International Fashion Fabric Exhibition, Interstoff, Los Angeles International Textile Show, Pitti Filati, and Yarn Fair International (Keiser & Garner, 2003). The fabric vendors at these shows frequently have prototype garments made to help sell their newest offerings (Keiser & Garner, 2003). The shows also feature an area in which trend forecasters can share their seasonal predictions, while seminars and speakers alert product developers to trends and new technology. By attending fabric fairs, designers and product developers can confirm developing trends, identify new resources, and order sample fabric yardage (Keiser & Garner, 2003).

Trade publications and magazines are another important source for preliminary research on new materials in the marketplace. *Women's Wear Daily* and *Bobbin* magazine are two of the periodicals that product developers rely on for information on fabric trends (Keiser & Garner, 2003). Fabric libraries and printed fabrics are other sources. Because prints are so expensive, many product developers hire their own graphic designers to develop exclusive prints for their lines. Because product developers have limited print budgets, product developers recolor or rescale the purchased prints or have motifs extracted to develop coordinating prints (Keiser & Garner, 2003). Usually, sourcing of fabric samples is carried out both domestically and internationally. Sourcing locations include New York and Los Angeles, as well as several European countries, India, Hong Kong, Pakistan, Taiwan, Japan, and Indonesia (Wickett et al., 1999).

As the color palette forecasted for a future season is translated to textiles, the fabric's texture, depth, and geometry will often determine a specific color's usefulness (Linton, 1994). Merle Lindby-Young, a color and materials specialist, mentioned that surface is a critical component in this mix and observed she could not separate the color and the surface of textiles. Color and finish together render a material appropriate for a given time (Linton, 1994).

Forecasters and product developers begin to forecast apparel **styles** about one year ahead of the retailing season. For them, inspiration for silhouettes and style details comes from a variety of sources. They gather information and research by attending fashion shows and trade events and by reviewing fashion news from online or print materials and broadcast sources. They also subscribe to design resources, shop and interpret the market, and meet with suppliers to determine the design direction that is right for their companies (Keiser & Garner, 2003). New, innovative styles and new shopping areas are featured in magazines such as *Women's Wear Daily, Vogue, Harper's Bazaar, Collezioni Donna,* and *In Style* and in industry newsletters (Keiser & Garner, 2003). Some magazines, such as *Vogue, Elle,* and *Cosmopolitan,* have different editions for different countries. It is valuable for trend forecasters to shop signature stores in the major fashion cities in which the designers are based. Forecasters must plan their trips carefully in order to hit the most relevant markets for particular seasons. For instance, junior product developers may shop the avant-garde markets of London, Paris, and Amsterdam. Bridge designers may be more influenced by designers' ready-to-wear collections in London, Paris, and Milan. Accessory designers look to innovative designers such as Gucci, Prada, and Dolce & Gabbana (Keiser & Garner, 2003). These sources are sifted for core concepts or trends. Then, the trends identified from various sources are translated to fit a company's identity and its customers' lifestyles and preferences for specific lines (Brannon, 2005). Finally, the elements are assembled into an actionable forecast to be used for line development by product category, price point, and retail concept (Brannon, 2005).

Trend services provide reports with immediate, in-depth sources of information about the collections (see Figure 3.6). The services work very quickly, publishing their reports on the Internet because publication in magazines take months. The reports often suggest changes in silhouettes and details. Some generate fashion sketches that incorporate a variety of ideas into single garments. These sketches are sometimes overdesigned, requiring subscribers to reinterpret the idea for their target market (Keiser & Garner, 2003). Many trend services also offer personalized services, such as designing, brand development, market research, feasibility studies, customer profile analyses, and branding imaging to help their clients develop products. They can perform these services on an individual consultation basis, or they may actually develop an entire line for a company (Frings, 2008).

First View, a fashion publication available on a fee basis with photos of the latest fashion collections from Paris, Milan, London, and New York, is one of a number of such Web sites (Frings, 2008). Video is another ideal medium for fashion reporting. *Videofashion News,* which offers collection coverage and behind-the-scenes designer interviews, appears regularly on the Style network, Cablevision's Metro TV. *Videofashion News* DVDs are also sold to stores, companies, and libraries.

Timing is a critical element of fashion. The right fashion, introduced too soon, quickly turns into a loss; however, carrying a silhouette or color beyond its fashion cycle is equally costly (Keiser & Garner, 2003). One example of manufacturers'

Figure 3.6 SS 2010 fashion show held in Sydney in Australia reported by EDITD.

Source: EDITD. Retrieved from http://editd.com/features/.

failure to read consumer demand on correct timing was the introduction of the midi skirt in the late 1960s and early 1970s. This misjudgment led to serious financial loss and business closures (Diane & Cassidy, 2005). Case 3.2 provides an example of a forecasting failure that caused Urban Outfitters a large financial loss.

CASE 3.2. AN EXAMPLE OF FORECASTING FAILURE—"URBAN OUTFITTERS, FASHION VICTIM," 2006

Urban Outfitters misjudged customers' tastes. Heather Fauland is a typical Urban Outfitters shopper. Usually clad in jeans and a witty t-shirt, the 21-year-old college student turns to them for the edgy fashion that sets her apart from mainstream teens, but since Christmas, their reliable look has changed. When stopping by Urban Outfitters, she dismissed the mannequins sporting tight leggings and a tank top worn over a button-down shirt over a sweater with odd cuts and capped sleeves. Fauland said, "I just don't seem to like their kind of edgy right now. It looks funny."

Urban Outfitters' success lies in its ability to pinpoint exactly what kind of edge its hip customers want, and judging by the past few months, the chain badly misjudged its shoppers' sensibilities. In the fall of 2005, Urban's buyers proved too quick to embrace new styles. Urban's customers were not willing to part with distressed jeans and peasant shirts in favor of '80s-style peg-legged pants and baggy V-shaped tops. Urban Outfitters was too aggressive, and now its fashion faux pas is beginning to hurt the bottom line. Net income had climbed an average annual 44 percent since 2003, hitting $131 million in 2005 on sales of $1.1 billion, but recently, inventory has started to pile up. As a result, first-quarter earnings plunged 26 percent, and the chain's stock skidded to 15.95, a fifty-two-week low.

Compounding Urban's woes was a miscalculation at another of its apparel chains, Anthropologie Inc. In September 2005 Anthropologie's airy French countryside interiors were eclipsed by goth clothes leaning toward the theatrical: high necks, dark colors, odd oversize buttons. When consumers did not bite, Anthropologie rapidly retooled, stocking October shelves with staples such as basic pants and long-sleeved t-shirts, but by that time, consumers already had what they needed for the season.

In retail, "it is hard to be on the top of the heap for a long period of time," says Mary Brett Whitfield, a senior vice-president at research firm Retail Forward Inc. in Columbus, Ohio. "What's hot one moment can easily be not [the next]." The company will need to make smarter bets about style, helping its shoppers to be in fashion, but not ahead of fashion.

Source

Urban Outfitters: Fashion victim. (2006, July 17). *Bloomberg Businessweek*. Retrieved from http://www.businessweek.com/magazine/content/06_29/b3993067.htm

It will be increasingly difficult to forecast trends in the future as they become more diverse. In the past, a forecasting company could make a profit by identifying the one major trend; now it is hard to identify all of the diverse trends that develop (Lee, 2009). A shorter fashion cycle makes forecasting even harder. However, trend analysis and forecasting will be just as important because there will be a need to guide the development of continuously evolving products. With the proliferation of new products and shorter product life cycles, it may be impossible to obtain as much history as a forecast analyst needs for good model building. In personal computers and consumer electronics, for example, product life cycles are typically three to eighteen months. Fashion apparel items sell for just one season. On the other hand, with the development of new technology, the quantity and quality of data will continue to increase. For example, retail point-of-sale (POS) data is now widely available, making product consumption patterns available to consumer product manufacturers. Web site traffic is another new data point, and several services now provide weather-related data, economic indicators, and other types of information that forecasting models can readily use.

In the future, more companies that produce various fashion products such as cars, electronics, and interiors will depend on trend services than ever before. In the past, apparel and accessories companies were the trend services' major clients. However, the trend service firms will face a challenge because consumers will increasingly have access to more and more information over the Internet. For example, consumers can now see, in real time, fashion shows for the next season as they take place in Europe. Consumers have become more refined and savvy. With increased access to information, anyone can analyze trends to some extent. Therefore, forecasting firms will do consulting for planning, execution of line developments, and branding in conjunction with trending, which will differentiate them as experts (Lee, 2009).

Chapter Summary

- Fashion forecasting process begins about two years in advance of the retailing season for new products. Broadly, this process encompasses three components: environment, market, and product. First, the environment is scanned to search for current and near future trends in the economic, political, social, and cultural arenas. Understanding the long-term direction of the society can also benefit fashion professionals. Second, market research on consumers, competing companies, and sales records is conducted. In the final step, the transition of previous products over time is analyzed and the color, textile, and styles of new products for the next season are forecasted.

- Two types of fashion forecasting are used: short-term forecasting, which envisions trends one to two years in the future and focuses on new product features such as color, textile, and style, and long-term forecasting, which predicts trends five or more years out and focuses on the directions of the fashion industry with regard to materials, design, production, and retailing. Long-term forecasts contribute to a fashion firm's development strategies and help it make decisions related to repositioning or extending product lines, initiating new businesses, and reviving brand images.
- In developing a new collection of apparel products, fashion professionals first select the color palette. Color forecasting is conducted from two to two and a half years in advance of the retailing season for new products. The decision about a seasonal color palette is the basis for dyeing yarns and fabric design for all styles in the line.
- Fiber producers and mills start projecting fabric trends eighteen months ahead of the retailing season. The task of researching seasonal fabrics goes on simultaneously with color research and the determination of a color story. Many services that provide color forecasts also offer fabric forecasts. These sources alert a product developer to new technology, fibers, blends, and finishes by providing descriptions, swatches, and sketches of possible applications.
- Forecasters and product developers begin forecasting apparel styles about one year ahead of the retailing season. For them, inspiration for silhouettes and style details comes from a variety of sources. They gather information and research by attending fashion shows and trade events and by reviewing fashion news from online or print materials and from broadcasting sources. They also subscribe to trend services and design resources and shop the stores in fashion centers.

Key Terms

- Analysis
- Awareness
- Color
- Environment
- Faith Popcorn
- Fashion forecasting methods
- Fashion forecasting process
- First View
- Information gathering
- Interpretation
- John Naisbitt
- Long-term forecasting
- Megatrend
- Observation
- Product development
- Product evolution
- Recognizing patterns
- Short-term forecasting
- Sociocultural context
- Style
- Synthesis
- Textiles
- Trade show
- Trend analysis
- Trend service
- Zeitgeist: the spirit of the time

Questions for review and discussion

1. What demographic changes do you expect in the consumer market in the next five to ten years? What demographic groups will be dominant in the market? How will the demographic factors influence future trends in the fashion industry, including apparel styles and consumption behaviors? How can the industry respond to these changes effectively?

2. Color has been identified as the most important design factor when consumers choose an apparel style. Discuss the differences in color preferences across continents in the world (e.g., North America, Europe, and Asia). You can choose specific countries to compare if you prefer. In addition, compare the differences in preference across areas within the United States (e.g., the East, Northeast, West, South, Pacific Northwest, and Midwest). Provide some examples from your observations or experiences.

3. What will be the future of fashion forecasting? Will it be needed more or less in the future? Why? What will influence the level of need? How will the shorter fashion cycle affect forecasting? Are there any factors that will make forecasting activities more or less difficult? Will the development of technology affect forecasting activities in the future? How? Do you envision any changes in the trend forecasting business in the future?

Suggested Readings

Diane, T., & Cassidy, T. (2005). *Color forecasting*. Oxford, UK: Blackwell Publishing.
Kim, E., & Johnson, K. K. P. (2007). The U.S. apparel industry: Futuring with undergraduate apparel majors. *Clothing & Textiles Research Journal, 25*(4), 283–306.
Kim, E., & Johnson, K. K. P. (2009). Forecasting the U.S. fashion industry with industry professionals. Part 1: Materials and design. *Journal of Fashion Marketing and Management, 13*(2), 256–267.
Kim, E., & Johnson, K. K. P. (2009). Forecasting the U.S. fashion industry with industry professionals. Part 2: Production and retailing. *Journal of Fashion Marketing and Management, 13*(2), 268–278.
Linton, H. (1994). *Color forecasting*. New York: Van Nostrand Reinhold.

References

Brannon, E. L. (2005). *Fashion forecasting* (2nd ed.). New York: Fairchild Publications.
Diane, T., & Cassidy, T. (2005). *Color forecasting*. Oxford, UK: Blackwell Publishing.
Eckman, M., Damhorst, M. L., & Kadolph, S. J. (1990). Toward a model of in-store purchase decision process: consumer use of criteria for evaluating women's apparel. *Clothing & Textiles Research Journal, 8*(2), 13–22.
Ferla, R. L. (2010, February 19). Fashion's military invasion rolls on. *The New York Times*. Retrieved from http://www.nytimes.com/2010/02/21/fashion/21military.html
Fiore, A. M., & Kimle, P. A. (1997). *Understanding aesthetics for the merchandising and design professional*. New York: Fairchild Publications.
Frings, G. S. (2008). *Fashion from concept to consumer* (9th ed.). Upper Saddle River, NJ: Pearson Prentice Hall.
Gaskill, L. R. (1992). Toward a model of retail product development: A case study analysis. *Clothing & Textiles Research Journal, 10*(4), 17–24.
Hope, A., & Walch, M. (1990). *The color compendium*. New York: Van Nostrand Reinhold.

Johne, F. A., & Snelson, P. A. (1990). *Successful product development: Lessons for American and British firms*. Oxford: Blackwell Publishing.

Keiser, S. J., & Garner, M. B. (2003). *Beyond design*. New York: Fairchild Publications.

Lamkins, C. (2010). The 2010 color forecast. Retrieved from http://www.cccfcs.com/uploads/Interior%20Design/ID%2009/Lamkins-12-09%20-Color-final.pdf

Lauer, D. A., & Pentak, S. (2008). *Design basics* (7th ed.). Belmont, CA: Thomson Wadsworth.

Lee, C. (2009). An interview with Chungmin Lee, the CEO of First View Korea—PFIN by Eundeok Kim on July 2, 2009.

Linton, H. (1994). *Color forecasting*. New York: Van Nostrand Reinhold.

Moschis, G. P., Lee, E., Mathur, A., & Strautman, J. (2000). *The maturing marketplace: Buying habits of baby boomers and their parents*. Westport, CT: Quorum Books.

Popcorn, F. (1991). *The Popcorn report: Faith Popcorn on the future of your company, your world, your life*. New York: Doubleday.

Sproles, G. B. (1979). *Fashion: Consumer behavior toward dress*. Minneapolis: Burgess Publications.

Sproles, G. B., & Burns, L. D. (1994). *Changing appearances: Understanding dress in contemporary society*. New York: Fairchild Publications.

Szustek, A. (2009, February 4). J. Crew's uptick: The "Obama factor" or recession-conscious fashion? *Finding Dulcinea*. Retrieved from http://www.findingdulcinea.com/news/business/2009/feb/J-Crew-s-Uptick-The–Obama-Factor-or-Recession-Conscious-Fashion-.html

Urban Outfitters: Fashion victim. (2006, July 17). *Bloomberg Businessweek*. Retrieved from http://www.businessweek.com/magazine/content/06_29/b3993067.htm

Wickett, J. L., Gaskill, L. R., & Damhorst, M. L. (1999). Apparel retail product development: Model testing and expansion. *Clothing & Textiles Research Journal, 17*(1), 21–35.

4

THE ROLE OF FASHION INDUSTRY PROFESSIONALS IN TREND DEVELOPMENT AND FORECASTING

Objectives

- Understand the roles of fashion industry professionals in creating and supporting trends
- Understand the forecasting activities of major companies
- Understand forecasting as a team effort

The roles of fashion industry professionals in creating and supporting trends

Fashion trends and forecasting do not happen overnight, nor are they created by a small number of people who have a special ability to see the future. Rather, they involve various professionals in the fashion industry who engage in a continual, systematic, and analytical process that explains changes in society and in behavior (O'Brien, 2003). Forecasting companies and developers collect information related to culture, the economy, politics, and technology that may influence future trends. The staffs of forecasting companies travel all around the world, looking at cultural indicators that indicate new ways of living, shopping, and designing, gleaning information from books, arts, music, movies, fashion, architecture, restaurants, and nightspots. They also examine published articles and public records and talk to experts and scholars in related areas, such as sociologists, economists, scientists, and marketers. Using various types of research, forecasters identify changes in consumer characteristics, such as age, educational level, attitudes, and preferences. On the basis of their analysis of these changes, they develop trend forecasting for professionals in various areas, who use the information in making decisions about product design (Tay, 1998). For instance, apparel designers use trend forecasts related to colors, fabrics, and silhouettes to develop merchandise, which can fit their target consumers' preferences for upcoming seasons.

Consumers are influenced by fashion trends selected by fashion magazines and buyers, called gatekeepers, and promoted by advertisers and visual merchandisers, called promoters. For instance, fashion magazine editors select new trends or hot styles and introduce them to consumers. Buyers also choose merchandise that will appeal to their target customers. Once gatekeepers select new fashions, advertisers, stylists, and visual merchandisers promote them to increase consumer awareness, familiarity, and observability and to enhance the aesthetic value of the newly introduced products (Fiore & Kimle, 1997).

Think about the trend colors of the past season. You were able to find similar colors in almost every fashion merchandise category, including apparel, sunglasses, shoes, handbags, cosmetics, and accessories. It was easy to find advertisements and magazines showing these colors in fashion, while visual merchandisers displayed the trend colors in their windows. Although color organizations and forecasting companies initially create trend forecasting, every sector in the fashion industry shares and promotes the information. This chapter introduces various categories of professionals (developers, gatekeepers, and promoters) and explains their roles in creating and supporting trends. It also addresses trend forecasting as an integrated process, involving the efforts of a team drawn from a variety of fashion sectors.

The roles of developers, gatekeepers, and promoters

Developers

Developers are "professionals involved in the creation of the product, from initiating and contributing ideas, presenting the ideas, through perfecting the design, and ending with the completion of production" (Fiore, 2010, p. 16). In the fashion industry, developers include apparel designers, product developers, colorists, and textile artists. For instance, an apparel designer will look for design inspiration, develop design or line concepts, and design individual apparel items; a colorist will create color concepts and color combinations for fabrics. For all of these professionals, one of the most important inspirational sources is forecasting materials. Therefore, fashion trend forecasters can also be considered as developers because they contribute ideas to the creative process. For example, if fashion forecasts suggest a trend toward military-inspired looks, designers will use design components such as olive green camouflage patterns, patch pockets, and other utilitarian details. As we see later in this chapter, trend forecasters also help gatekeepers and promoters, because these professionals also use trend materials developed by forecasters.

Trend forecasting services

While fashion trends cover various design elements, such as color, styles, silhouettes, and fabrics, forecasting begins by determining the trend colors of the season. There are two leading professional color organizations in the United

States: The Color Association of the United States (CAUS) and the Color Marketing Group (CMG).

The Color Association of the United States (CAUS) is a nonprofit organization, based in New York. As noted in chapter 1, CAUS, originally called the Textile Color Card Association of America (TCCA), was founded in 1915 and issued its first forecast in 1917 (Brannon, 2010). The membership of this organization is composed of professionals in the areas of apparel, textiles, interiors, retailing, education, and automobiles, among others. For each area of focus, such as interiors or women's, men's, and youth apparel, a committee of five to ten is formed. CAUS members serve on these committees, depending on their interests and expertise. The committee meets twice a year to select twenty-four trend colors for women's, men's, and youth apparel and forty-four trend colors for interiors, and these colors will dominate the market for the next two years. With the cost of membership, all members receive a forecast package for each season, consisting of color samples (dyed silk or wool thread), a written report on the rationale behind the selection of the colors, and a CD of inspiration images (The Color Association of the United States, n.d.).

The **Color Marketing Group (CMG),** founded in 1962, is an international nonprofit association based in Alexandria, Virginia. Members, representing companies in the textiles, apparel, and home furnishing industries, are from more than twenty countries. CMG members meet twice a year to develop a color forecast nineteen months prior to the selling season in such product categories as apparel, home furnishings, and automobiles. Members develop individual color forecasts, considering various influences and trends that each member identifies within its industry. Then, more than four hundred CMG members from all over the world meet at two international conferences to identify color trends. During the conferences, CMG members discuss the color trends and changes in society, culture, technology, the economy, the environment, politics, and demographics for different groups. A steering committee synthesizes the discussions and the color forecasts offered by all members and develops the final forecast (Color Marketing Group, n.d.).

In addition to CAUS and CMG, which are nonprofit organizations that focus on color forecasting, there are a number of profit-making forecasting firms. They provide comprehensive trend forecasts, including colors, fabrics, and silhouettes, as well as merchandising and consulting services, to their clients. A sample of the major players follows.

The Doneger Group, founded in 1946 and based in New York, is one of the major sources of global market trends and merchandising strategies. It provides various services, including trend forecasting, merchandising (product development), and buying, to its clients. (The practice of buying services is discussed later in this chapter; see the section "Gatekeepers"). Doneger Creative Services (DCS) is the company's trend forecasting division. It offers color and fabric directions to its clients eighteen months prior to the selling season, as well as up-to-date retail, street, and runway information and analysis. Here & There, a leader in the fashion forecasting industry, merged with DCS in 2006 to expand its services and provide clients with color, fabric, silhouette, and print trends (see Figure 4.1). In addition, it offers online reports of ready-to-wear and haute couture collections and images of the latest styles on the streets, in stores, and in store windows in cities in the United States, Europe, and Asia (The Doneger Group, n.d.).

One of the major phenomena in the area of fashion forecasting today is the growth of online forecasting companies. Although there are numerous online forecasting companies worldwide (see Table 4.1), Worth Global Style Network (WGSN) and Stylesight are known as the world's leading web-based forecasting companies.

The **Worth Global Style Network (WGSN),** established in 1998, has more than 2,500 clients and 35,000 users in eighty-one countries. WGSN has more than 200 teams with creative and editorial staff that travel the globe, researching and analyzing style trends, and a network of experienced writers, photographers, researchers, analysts, and trend spotters. WGSN covers 114 cities annually; London, New York,

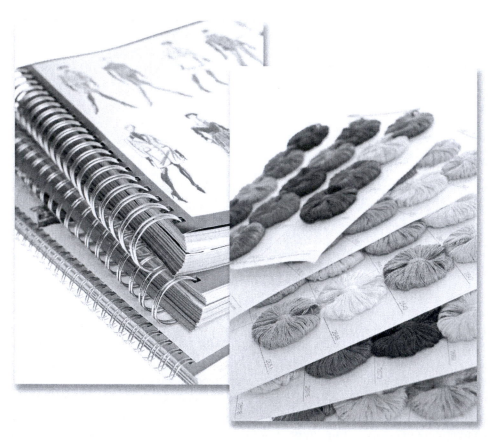

Figure 4.1 Doneger Creative Services (DCS) provides clients with forecasting materials, including color, fabric, and design trends.
Source: The Doneger Group.

Table 4.1 Online Trend Forecasting Services

Color Portfolio Inc. (www.colorfortfolio.com)	Texas, U.S.	Offers color and trend books and consulting services to apparel and interior companies.
Fashion Snoops (www.fashionsnoops.com)	New York, U.S.	Provides clients with international runway, trade show, and retail reports and trend forecasts in design themes, colors, silhouettes, graphics, and other details.
Infomat (www.infomat.com)	Paris, France	Provides clients with trend analysis; street style, store windows, runway, trade show, and consumer trend reports; and access to more than 350,000 international showrooms, retailers, and manufacturers.
Milou Ket Styling & Design (www.milouket.com)	Purmerend, Netherlands	Provides clients with trend books, including Interiors, Innovationlab, Interior Colours, and Women Trends; offers consulting services on market position, image, target groups, competition, and company strategy.
Mudpie Design Ltd. (www.mpdclick.com)	London, U.K.	Provides clients with trend book publication, industry news, consulting, and downloadable graphic, print, and flat sketches, specifically focusing on youth/ children market.
NellyRodi™ (www.nellyrodi.com)	Paris, France	Provides designers in the textile, packaging, automotive, and cosmetic industries with unique insight into future consumer trends; offers marketing and sociological analysis of consumer behavior and consulting services.
The Future Laboratory (www.thefuturelaboratory.com)	London, U.K.	Provides trend forecasting, consumer insight, and brand strategy to clients in retailing, technology, automotive, food, fashion, and other creative industries; offers consulting services such as brand strategy.
Trend Bible (www.trendbible.co.uk)	Newcastle upon Tyne, U.K.	Provides trend books for the home interiors and kid's lifestyle sectors; offers consulting services for clients in the United Kingdom and the United States.

and Paris are covered monthly. Information collected from these cities is delivered to clients in the form of weekly and monthly reports. WSGN also provides in-depth analysis of trends twenty-four months ahead, forward trend tracking twelve months ahead, and close-to-season overviews three to six months ahead of the selling season. WGSN forecast services cover a wide range of areas and topics in the fashion industry, with 4.8 million images and 600,000 pages of contents. Through its eighteen directories, the Web site provides information on color, fabric, and silhouette forecasts ("Trends"), key events from around the world ("News"), images from major collections ("Cat Walks"), yarn, fabric, and garment trade shows ("Trade Shows"), textile news and innovative textiles ("Materials"), and eight thousand monthly updated photographs of products from all around the world ("What's in Store") (Worth Global Style Network, n.d.).

Stylesight, founded in 2003, provides its services to one thousand clients, including Macy's, Target, Victoria's Secret, and Liz Claiborne (Miller, 2008). Based in New York, Stylesight has more than sixty trend reporters and forecasters who have extensive experiences in the areas of fashion design, trend analysis, forecasting, reporting, merchandising, and apparel manufacturing. One of the great features of the company's Web site is the image library search engine, called Stylesight Search, which allows clients to access more than five million inspirational images, zoom in to see details, download and print images for use in storyboards, organize images into folders according to the specific seasonal idea, and share folders with colleagues. Stylesight Search consists of images categorized into Designer Collections, Street Fashions, Vintage Styles, Retail Stores, Celebrity Fashions, Denims, Color, and Trade Shows. Stylesight's forecast services cover apparel for women, men, youth, and children, as well as interiors. Its services provide information on color trends ("Color Premiere"), seasonal trends, inspirational images, cultural references ("Megatrend Seasonal Forecasts"), print and pattern trends ("Print & Graphics"), and in-depth research into product design ("Design Development") (Stylesight, n.d.) (see Figure 4.2).

Figure 4.2 Stylesight Search includes more than five million images that inspire the fashion, style, and trend industries.

Source: Stylesight.

Case 4.1 introduces an article that discusses how Stylesight can be used by various professionals in the fashion industry. Table 4.1 shows a variety of online forecasting companies worldwide. Through Activity 4.1 you may visit one of the Web sites, examine the services provided by the company, and share the information with your class mates.

CASE 4.1. IN-DEPTH WITH STYLESIGHT.COM

The premiere trend forecasting service and industry insiders' secret weapon, Stylesight.com is one big think tank of global fashion content, carrying tools and the newest of technologies all in one spot and all at your disposal. It is useful for every fashion professional you can think of. Designers, buyers, executives, journalists, stylists and everyone in between can benefit.

When I was a designer in New York City, I used tools on Stylesight.com such as *Forecast, Prints & Graphics, Market Intelligence, Speed to Market and Runway*. Stylesight. com gave me the foresight to design a collection that had all the correct elements for a marketable and exciting clothing line. The site inspired my color directions, trend directions, print directions and inspiring vintage details to boot. . . . You can play with every Pantone, create your color palette and design your collection with focus. *Color Play* can be useful to everyone, but it's essential for designers.

To be on top as a stylist, I would recommend using *Forecast, Futurist, Runway, Trend Watch, Vintage and Style Traveler* sections to pull ideas together for how to style clients. With an image library of over 4 million pictures to work with, play with and inspire, you can bring to the table sharp styling with a creative and cutting edge. Stylesight.com gives the market research and inspiration to help create groundbreaking ideas that are on top of the latest street trends.

But what if you're not a designer or stylist? What if you're a buyer? There are sections for buyers, too—encompassing men's, women's, and children's clothing as well as activewear, accessories and even denim, you can be on top of your business while exploring street to market trends and what's happening in other retail shops and showrooms around the world. Stylesight has *global* vision. As a buyer, the more you know about your market and market trends, the better you can plan your next season of buying.

Locally in Los Angeles, companies like Young, Fabulous & Broke, Linea Pelle, Inc., Kasil Jean, Forever 21, Chinese Launday and FIDM all use Stylesight. Big wigs use it, too. Companies like Target, Victoria's Secret, Sherwin Williams, and Abercrombie & Fitch all use it, too.

Laurie is an image consultant and celebrity stylist based in Los Angeles, California.

Source

Excerpts from Brucker, L. (2010, May 3). In-depth with stylesight.com. [Web log comment]. Retrieved from http://fashionablymarketing.me/2010/05/in-depth-with-stylesight-com/

ACTIVITY 4.1. PRESENTATION ON ONLINE TREND FORECASTING SERVICES

For this activity, students form groups with three or four (or more depending on class size) peers. Each group is assigned one of the online trend forecasting services listed in Table 4.1; it visits the Web site and develops a PowerPoint presentation to show to class. This presentation should include an introduction to the service and information provided by the Web site, accompanied by visual images. This activity may be announced to students before class so that they can develop their PowerPoint slides outside the classroom.

Merchandising and product development organizations

While the major role of forecasting companies is to provide trend forecasts in color, fabric, and silhouette trends for upcoming seasons to their retail clients, services provided by merchandising and product development organizations go even further and can include a brand concept or merchandise line development based on the trend forecasts. The leading merchandising and product development services are Henry Doneger Associates (HDA) and Tobe, which are divisions of The Doneger Group. On the basis of market trend research and a client's business analysis, the staff at HDA provides retail clients with merchandising suggestions, including new brand concepts and key items to include for the upcoming sales season (The Doneger Group, n.d.). For instance, if a client wants to develop a new jean line or improve its existing line, the HDA staff will conduct market research about the competition (e.g., identify competitors) and consumers (e.g., consumer characteristics, including demographic information and fashion preferences). In addition, it will analyze the client's business in terms of brand concept, merchandise, and price strategies. HDA then suggests a line concept, including colors, fabrics, and silhouettes; identifies key items; and provides detailed analyses to develop or improve the client's jean line.

While HDA is a merchandising service, Tobe is an international fashion and retail consulting service, providing clients with fashion and retail analyses, trend forecasting, product and brand development, merchandising and strategic planning, and market news. Since 1927, the **Tobe Report**, referred to as "the bible of the fashion industry" ("Color Trends . . . ," n.d.), has been one of the leading fashion consulting weekly publications for retailers. It contains information on current and coming trends—the best sellers that retailers are looking for, which are designated by specific style numbers, with the names of the producers and the wholesale prices (Jarnow & Dickerson, 1997).

Trade shows

Many fashion innovations are proposed at yarn and fabric shows, as introduced in chapter 3. Thus, these shows are also important inspirational sources for developers. Most trade shows in Europe and the United States are held twice yearly. At trade shows, a variety of yarn and fabric companies present their products in one location for a short period time so that they can be considered by fashion professionals from all over the world. Attendees consist of executives responsible for developing and purchasing fabrics in large quantities, designers looking for inspiration, forecasters seeking the signs of future trends for upcoming seasons, and the fashion press. Trade shows also offer attendees seminars and presentations on fashion trends in color, fabric, and silhouette. Two of the top yarn shows include Expofil (Paris, France) and Pitti Immagine Filati (Florence, Italy). Fabric shows include Premiere Vision (Paris, France), Ideacomo (Cernobbio, Italy), and Moda-In (Milan, Italy). Garment shows include Magic (originally held in Las Vegas) and the Canton trade show (Canton, China).

The best-known fabric trade show in the world is probably **Premiere Vision**, held twice a year, eleven to twelve months prior to the selling season. Premiere Vision is considered the most useful trade show among fashion professionals because it presents not only textiles but also color trends compiled by its panel members. About eighty panel members from all areas of the fashion industry work on the color ranges eighteen months ahead of the selling season (Diane & Cassidy, 2005). There are between 650 and 700 exhibitors, including fabric, print, knit, leather, fur, and embroidery/ribbon companies, from thirty countries (Premiere Vision, n.d.). Although it originally had its shows in Paris, Premiere Vision now also has shows in New York, Moscow, Shanghai, and Tokyo. About fifty thousand fashion professionals from 110 countries visit the show (McKelvey & Munslow, 2008).

Consumer research

Consumer research is an essential part of fashion forecasting because it allows forecasters to identify shifting consumer lifestyles and preferences and to anticipate future trends. Fashion companies also conduct consumer research to identify and understand their consumers, expose problems and opportunities, and make better decisions in product development, brand marketing, and retailing (Churchill & Iacobucci, 2005). The following example shows how consumer research can be successfully used by fashion companies.

In the late 1980s, Liz Claiborne, a women's wear brand, found that 40 percent of the female consumers in the United States wore size 14 or larger. Many of these consumers required a professional wardrobe, but they had been ignored by the fashion industry. On the basis of these consumer research findings, Liz Claiborne added a line specifically targeting the large-size career woman (Muller & Smiley, 1995).

There are two main types of consumer research techniques: qualitative and quantitative research. **Qualitative research** techniques are used to explore subjective opinions or perceptions of consumers—why consumers buy or do not buy a particular brand or product—whereas **quantitative research** is used to analyze and understand consumer preferences, beliefs, or attitudes—the general attitude of consumers toward a specific brand or product. While qualitative research techniques involve a relatively small number of consumers, quantitative research techniques use data collected from a large number of consumers. The most commonly used qualitative research techniques are focus groups, depth interviews, and projective techniques (Churchill & Iacobucci, 2005).

Focus group interviews are one of the most popular techniques in consumer research. Focus groups consist of a small number of consumers who are brought together to talk about topics of interest to the researcher in a group interview setting (Churchill & Iacobucci, 2005). Focus group interviews are used to understand both consumer behavior in general and consumer responses to specific products or brands. Forecasters may use focus group interviews to explore consumers' exercise behavior to develop a new product. For example, the Nike-iPod sports kit was developed to satisfy the needs of iPod users who also want to track their exercise information using the device; a sensor placed in a Nike shoe beneath the insole transfers exercise information (time, distance, pace, and calories burned) to the iPod receiver as the consumer runs.

Although focus groups vary in size, most include eight to twelve participants. Group discussions with fewer than eight participants may be easily dominated by a few participants who have strong opinions, which may result in frustration and boredom among other participants. Thus, researchers usually select and screen focus groups so that the groups are homogeneous in terms of their experiences in the topic area (Churchill & Iacobucci, 2005). In focus group interviews, the moderator plays a key role. The moderator needs to understand the research objectives and leads the discussion so that participants feel free to discuss their feelings, opinions, and experiences (Churchill & Iacobucci, 2005).

Depth interviews are similar to focus group interviews, but they involve one participant at a time—one-on-one interviews. The interviewer may lead the discussion by asking the participant a set of questions developed prior to the interview (i.e., a **structured interview**), or the interviewer may not have specific, predeveloped questions and instead may ask the participant to freely talk about the topic, spontaneously asking questions as the conversation goes (i.e., an **unstructured interview**) (Touliatos & Compton, 1988). Such interviews allow participants to answer questions in greater depth and involvement than do focus groups. Therefore, depth interviews are used to gain a deeper, richer understanding about consumers.

Projective techniques use prompts, such as incomplete sentences, word association tests, or images for storytelling. A participant is asked to complete the sentences or word association or to build a story around an image (Churchill & Iacobucci, 2005). These techniques are designed to make it easier for participants to express themselves and to disclose their inner motivations (Schiffman, Kanuk, & Wisenblit, 2010). For instance, if the researcher is using a word association technique, participants are given a list of words and asked, "What first comes to your mind when you see each word?" The responses to each of the keywords are examined to see what themes may be detected from the participant's word choices. This technique can be used by forecasters to identify consumer perceptions of a client's brand image (Churchill & Iacobucci, 2005). In Activity 4.2, try a projective technique to explore perceptions of specific apparel stores held by your classmates.

ACTIVITY 4.2. CONSUMER RESEARCH: PROJECTIVE TECHNIQUE

For this activity, students conduct in-class consumer research using a projective technique. Students should imagine that they are staff members of a merchandising service. To provide a client with merchandising suggestions (brand concept or product line development), they must first determine how consumers perceive the brand/store's image). The steps are as follows:

- Form groups of six or seven students.
- Have each group select one apparel store or brand.
- Have each student list words, phrases, or clauses associated with the store or brand. What comes to mind when you think of the store or brand? Think about the image of the store, which may include merchandise, store environment, advertisements, services, sales associates, and locations.
- Examine the words from all group members, and decide which themes emerge from the responses. Once themes are identified, categorize the responses according to the themes. For instance, you may come up with themes such as "young," "expensive," "casual," "limited selection," "pleasant store environment," and "appearance of sales associates." You may list responses such as "look young," "college students," and "young models in advertising" under the theme "young." Through this process, you can identify important associations related to the store or brand in customers' minds.
- On the basis of your findings, discuss the following questions:
- What is the most dominant theme?
- What are the mostly frequently mentioned words within each theme?
- Are there any surprising or unexpected findings?

One of the most commonly used quantitative research methods is the **survey**, in which an individual consumer answers a set of specific questions at one time. It is a useful method to investigate the demographic characteristics of a large number of consumers; surveys can ask about factors such as age, income, occupation, educational level, and family size and composition, and the responses can be used to classify individuals into market segments (Blackwell, Minard, & Engel, 2001). Merchandising or consulting services may use a survey technique to investigate consumers' demographic characteristics for specific brands. This information helps a company determine whether the target consumers identified by the company are actually its consumers. Researchers may present the same questions to the same group of people over time to track changes in consumers' attitudes, opinions, or preferences. This is called a panel study and is used to investigate changes in consumers' brand perception over time.

Consumer segmentation refers to "the process of identifying a group of people similar in one or more ways, based on a variety of characteristics and behaviors"

(Blackwell et al., 2001, p. 39). These characteristics may include age, income, life-style, and location. Forecasters or merchandising consultants collect consumer information through research they do themselves or that is completed by other sources (e.g., government agencies). They then use the information to formulate different consumer segments and provide clients suggestions related to a brand or line development; for instance, Abercrombie & Fitch, abercrombie, and Ruehl No. 925 belong to one company but target different consumer segments.

There are several factors (geographic, demographic, and lifestyle) that can be used to segment consumers into groups (Levy & Weitz, 2009). **Geographic segmentation** clusters consumers according to where they live. Consumers' geographic locations may influence their fashion adoption or preferences. For instance, consumers living in southern states prefer brighter colors and own more summer outfits because of the longer duration of warm weather. **Demographic segmentation** clusters consumers according to age, gender, income, ethnicity, or education. Consumer groups that are classified according to age are called age cohorts. People in the same age cohort tend to share common experiences and participate in similar cultural and social events and, therefore, are likely to share similar beliefs, attitudes, and behaviors. **Lifestyle segmentation,** also called **psychographic segmentation,** involves the formulation of groups on the basis of how consumers live, how they spend their time and money, what kinds of activities they enjoy, and what preferences, opinions, or worldviews they hold. Lifestyle segmentation is particularly useful because one's lifestyle directly affects one's behaviors as a consumer (Solomon & Rabolt, 2009) and because lifestyle is seen as a better predictor of consumer behavior than demographic variables (Levy & Weitz, 2009).

Competitive analysis

Fashion companies develop their merchandise on the basis of trend forecasts. However, the information does not necessarily guarantee their success in the market. Companies also need to understand environmental factors and market conditions, including their competitors. The main outcome of **competitive analysis** is to provide a company with a **competitive advantage.** Having a competitive advantage means that consumers decide to purchase a particular brand or product from one's firm because it offers better value than the other options. Value can come from a brand that is in some way more desirable or from product features, price, store environment, location, or service. Whereas **competitors** can easily copy some features that lead to a competitive advantage (e.g., they can match a lower price), other features are more sustainable (i.e., not easily copied). A **sustainable competitive advantage** refers to value-creating features that are not easily imitated by competitors and that, therefore, can be maintained over a period of time (Levy & Weitz, 2009). For instance, having a strong, positive brand image that captures the lifestyle of the target market may create a sustainable competitive advantage for a firm. Abercrombie & Fitch has built a strong image by consistently projecting its brand identity through every element of its business, such as products, store design, visual merchandising, and advertising. Being at the cutting edge of trends may create a sustainable advantage for firms because their product or brand image helps set consumers apart from their peers; on the other hand, some brands are good at sustaining classic trends, which are longer lasting and may offer a customer better economic value than cutting-edge products. To develop a sustainable competitive advantage, a firm must do a competitive analysis, identifying their competitors and their competitor's offerings and predicting competitors' responses to the market (Amit, Domowitz, & Fershtman, 1988). Through competitive analysis, forecasters and merchandising consultants provide suggestions to clients about how they can effectively differentiate their brands and products from those of their competitors.

A competitive analysis involves the collection of data related to competitors, environmental factors, and market conditions and the analysis of those data. In today's competitive marketplace, it is important for companies to be aware of their current and potential competitors, as well as their performance in the market. Companies should identify their direct competitors (those who sell the same product to the same customers in the same distribution) and their indirect competitors (those who sell alternatives). A company's current competitors will not necessarily be its competitors in the future. For instance, Gap has struggled because of increasing competition from fast-fashion companies, such as H&M and Zara (Lee, 2008; Poulter, 2005), which were not considered its direct competitors in the past. Merchandising and consulting services should be familiar with their clients' brands' competitors and provide them with merchandising suggestions, particularly in term of the competitors' pricing; merchandise, promotion, and distribution strategies; and strengths and weaknesses (Brannon, 2010; Levy & Weitz, 2009).

Competitive environmental analysis aims to identify major factors that influence the company's and competitors' market positions. Environmental factors consist of technological, economic, regulatory, and social changes (Levy & Weitz, 2009). Examining the changes in these factors and their effects is important for forecasters as well as for fashion firms because these are major factors that influence fashion change, as discussed in chapter 1.

Market analysis helps a company identify market trends, shifts in consumer preferences, and changes in competitors' strategies, all of which may influence the future plans of the business. As mentioned earlier, forecasters need to understand changes in market and consumer preferences to anticipate the market's future direction. Changes in main customer segments (e.g., age range, income levels, lifestyle) (Brannon, 2010) are critical for fashion firms, which need to understand these factors in order to plan their brand and merchandise lines in the future. For instance, if a company is targeting younger consumers, it may want to know the future growth of this consumer segment so that it can anticipate sales in the future. Also, the company may want to know the average income level of its consumer segment to make decisions about retail prices.

Although it is essential for companies to collect information regarding competitors' business activities to be competitive in the marketplace, some information-gathering activities are not legal and are regarded as unethical practices. The Intellectual Property Owners Association (IPO) provides guidelines that companies should follow to meet the highest ethical standards in competitive information gathering (Nolan, 2007):

- Espionage: **Industrial espionage** occurs when competitive information is collected in unlawful ways. Companies must not engage in any form of espionage regarding competitors, such as electronic eavesdropping, secret copying of files, or stealing documents from competitor's employees or agents.
- Using public sources: Companies may collect competitive information from public sources, advertisements, and online services. However, they must avoid seeking or obtaining information directly from competitors and refrain from any discussion with employees of a competitor concerning prices, terms or conditions of costs, or production quotas.
- Deceptive practices: Companies must not engage in deceptive activities to acquire information about competitors. These activities include misrepresenting one's identity for the purpose of seeking information.

Gatekeepers

Gatekeepers are professionals who filter the overflow of information and influence the products that are finally offered to consumers (Fiore & Kimle, 1997; Solomon & Rabolt, 2009). They are not paid to promote the products by the companies that produce the products (Fiore, 2010). *The New York Times* presents reviews of professionals in the areas of books, movies, music, dining and wine, and fashion and style. These reviews can increase or decrease consumers' curiosity about the product or service and influence their choices. In the fashion industry, professionals, such as buying offices, retail buyers, and fashion editors for consumer publications (e.g., *Vogue*) and industry publications (e.g., *Women's Wear Daily*), play a role selecting new fashions and introducing them to actual consumers.

Buying offices, retail buyers, fashion magazine editors, and bloggers

Almost every large retailer is affiliated with an independent buying office in the United States (Dickerson, 2002). For retailers outside New York City, buying offices assist in the buying process, particularly when the buyers cannot physically be in New York during the fashion weeks. For instance, The Doneger Group, the largest independent apparel buying office in the United States (Dickerson, 2002), offers clients buying services through its Carol Hoffman division. Carol Hoffman serves women's specialty retailers in the contemporary, better, bridge, designer, and couture markets. The staff at Carol Hoffman continuously informs clients of fashion, price, and new vendors and merchandise; arranges meetings and visits to vendors' showrooms for clients; and sometimes accompanies visiting buyers to vendors' showrooms, providing on-the-spot advice about orders. In addition, the staff evaluates vendors' lines, identifies new and important items for different clients, and makes suggestions about special and trendy items in buying situations (The Doneger Group, n.d.). It is critical for buying offices to be familiar with trend forecasting so that it can offer clients meaningful suggestions and position them as market leaders.

Retail buyers have the ultimate responsibility for selecting new fashion merchandise from the vast number of resources available (Diamond & Pintel, 2001). During market weeks, retail buyers visit various vendors to purchase merchandise that will satisfy their customers' needs and wants. Thus, buyers consider their target customers' preferences as well as their future preferences, not the buyer's personal preferences. For instance, buyers of Belk know that skinny jeans will be in fashion for the upcoming season. However, they may not purchase those jeans because Belk targets middle-aged, somewhat conservative customers; hence, skinny jean styles are not likely to be accepted by their customers. On the other hand, buyers from Neiman Marcus or Saks Fifth Avenue will definitely purchase various skinny jean styles because these stores target fashion-forward customers.

The **editors** of fashion magazines and newspapers are important gatekeepers in the fashion industry because many consumers learn about new fashion trends through these publications. *Vogue*, first published in 1892, introduces and reviews new fashion trends, products, and designer lines for a wide audience. *Vogue* editors introduce hot items for the season. For example, the fall 2010 issue of *Vogue* showed "the season's key fashion trends" for swimwear (Burke, 2010). Case 4.2 showcases the comments of *Vogue*'s editors about the new fashion trends for Fall/Winter 2010 and Spring 2011. Appearing in a magazine that creates awareness, increases prestige, and evaluates trends, *Vogue*'s choices and editorial comments influence consumers' adoption of the trends and products.

CASE 4.2. THE ROLE OF THE FASHION EDITOR AS A GATEKEEPER: INTRODUCING MAJOR TRENDS

In the May issue, *Vogue* editor Tonne Goodman suggests several styles as fashion trends for fall/winter 2010: Gibson girl, patriot, flapper (the 1920s young woman), bohemian, and Hollywood screen siren styles. First, the article says, "The GIBSON GIRL rode out toward independence on her liberation vehicle of choice, the bicycle, way back in the 1890s— and her image of vitality reverberates today in the broad and confident shoulders of, for instance, a Ralph Lauren cashmere sweater" (Goodman, 2010, p. 187). The editor then suggests PATRIOT as one of the major fashion themes in fall/winter 2010, saying that ".embrace of utilitarianism remains the core value of military-inspired looks in 2010" (p. 187).

Source

Goodman, T. (2010, May). Rebel, rebel. *Vogue*, 187.

Jessica Kerwin Jenkins (2010) identifies two major trends influencing Spring 2011 fashion: Camden (the epicenter of London street fashion, selling crafts and various styles of clothing, such as punk, Gothic, and hippie styles) and greenmarket. The editor lists studded biker jackets, slashed and safety-pinned t-shirts, ripped-up denim, flashes of Day-Glo, brothel-creepers, chopped-up bangs, and tattoos as fashion trend components or inspirations for Spring 2011. The article says, "After watching the seventh reference to 'street' fashion rising through the shows in London and Paris—not to mention what the most *on it* attendees were doing to their hair, makeup, jewelry, and footwear—it was hard not to wonder: Have they all been to Camden Market?" (p. 188). The article also addresses a fashion trend toward green, focusing on the rise of earthily luxurious accessories. "Michael Kors's ode to California included easy living American sportswear, from slouchy sweaters to khakis, great crocodile and cork sandals, and an enormous leather-handled straw tote" (p. 190). Other examples provided by the editor include Raf Simons's oversized striped tote at Jill Sander and Ferragamo's straw bucket bag.

Source

Jenkins, J. K. (2010, December). Market forces. *Vogue*, 188–190.

The editors of *Women's Wear Daily* may be the most important gatekeepers for fashion designers. The publication reviews and publicizes designers' new collections each season. *The New York Times* reported, "but it was news, and a sense of the new in fashion, that gave *Women's Wear Daily* its provocative edge, and that could make or break a designer" (Horyn, 1999, p. 4). Another article showed the influence of *Women's Wear Daily* as a gatekeeper and the importance of its reviews to designers: "The next day [of the Yves Saint Laurent's fashion show in Paris], a review of the Saint Laurent showing appeared not on page 1, where the paper usually reviews eminent designers, but on page 12. That, too, was a sign: the page 12 placement meant war" (Gross, 1987, p. 20).

Due to advances in Internet technologies, **bloggers** have emerged as a new type of gatekeeper. In its recent issue, *Vogue* introduced nine bloggers influential in fashion, discussing today's blogging phenomenon. The article says,

> No one, least of all the global fashion industry, could have ever predicted just how many people would be sufficiently interested in looking at stylistic gestures uploaded minutes after they were shot, or that those making them would attain celebrity status. No one had grasped the huge constituency with only one thing on its mind: What are Sasha Pivovarova/Anna dello Russo/Vanessa Traina, et al wearing today? All that has changed. Blogging can command a profile in the fashion world, bringing a certain kind of power and privilege. (Holgate, 2010, p. 514)

One of the bloggers introduced in the article is Tommy Ton, who started his blog, Jak & Jil, in 2005, photographing and introducing fashion-forward, trendy shoes. He says,

> It's more interesting to see heels like that walking on sand or on cobblestones than on a designer's runway. What I want to do is document personal style because that's what people are really interested in. (Holgate, 2010, p. 514)

These days, for fashion-conscious consumers, fashion editors, and stylists, it is as essential to read Ton's blog as it is to view the shows during a collection's launch if one wants to be up to date on shoe trends (Holgate, 2010).

Sales forecasting as a gatekeeping process

Zara's designers create about forty thousand new designs annually, and ten thousand of them are actually selected for production (Ferdow, Lewis, & Machuca, 2004). To select ten thousand final designs from among the forty thousand candidates, executives and designers consider various factors, such as the preferences of their target customers and the fashion trends of the selling season. Most importantly, they consider the salability of the designs—how much profit the designs could generate. Forecasting the sales of staple merchandise categories, such as laundry detergent, is relatively easy and accurate because these goods have a long life cycle with steady sales. Buyers in these merchandise categories typically predict their future sales on the basis of sales history. However, **sales forecasting** for fashion merchandise is challenging because most of the items in the category are new and highly seasonal and have a short life cycle (Levy & Weitz, 2009). Sales forecasting for fashion merchandise is especially difficult because styles have different life cycles (fad, fashion, and classic), so it is extremely hard for executives to predict when sales peaks will occur, as discussed in chapter 1.

Sales forecasting for fashion merchandise can be achieved by analyzing various types of information, such as sales history; using trend forecasting services; and talking to vendors and experts (Brannon, 2010; Levy & Weitz, 2009). This information can be analyzed by various techniques. Although many fashion designs are new, so that they have previous sales information, some styles have been repeatedly produced for more than one season. For instance, cardigan sweaters and black dresses are basic items for many women's apparel stores and are introduced every season with minor changes. In this case, executives generate accurate sales forecasting by reviewing previous sales data (Levy & Weitz, 2009). This technique is called a **time-series** analysis. Using this technique, executives can see patterns in sales history (e.g., an annual pattern of increasing and decreasing sales that corresponds with the seasons) and develop a forecast based on these patterns.

Other techniques commonly used to analyze past sales data are **correlation and regression techniques.** Correlation and regression techniques are statistical analyses used to examine whether or not there is a relationship between two variables. For instance, if a company has increased the number of sales associates over the years to improve service quality and, in turn, sales, executives may want to statistically test whether the increasing number of sales associates actually contributed significantly to an increase in sales so that they know whether to invest in sales associates in the future. Time-series, correlation, and regression techniques are quantitative techniques because these techniques use numerical values (e.g., number of sales associates, number of sales).

Vendors are important information sources for executives. Proprietary information about a vendor's marketing plan, such as promotions, will have a significant influence on sales. Also, vendors are knowledgeable about market trends for the merchandise categories with which they deal on a daily basis (Levy & Weitz, 2009). Thus, information from vendors about their marketing plans and market trends is useful for executives as they develop sales forecasting.

Finally, to develop sales forecasting, an executive may discuss ideas with in-house experts who are knowledgeable about market, consumer, product, and other environmental factors that influence sales. In addition, he or she may have a group of executives, salespeople, or outside experts, such as finance and marketing experts, with whom to discuss sales forecasting (Brannon, 2010). These activities use interview formats, which are qualitative techniques. Qualitative techniques are often used to adjust forecasts derived from quantitative techniques and to anticipate sales for new products without sales history.

Sales records, such as **point-of-sales (POS) data**, are an essential source of information for forecasting future sales down to the SKU (stock-keeping-unit). In apparel merchandise, a SKU means a particular color, size, and style (e.g., a pair of size 8 dark-blue skinny jeans). POS data are captured by a POS scanner as transactions occur. This transaction information is sent to the company's system. Executives (managers, buyers, or merchandisers) access the information to analyze the sales of their merchandise. The transaction data tell them which trends are being accepted by consumers and which ones are not. Also, POS data help executives determine when and how much to reorder or when to reduce prices if sales are slower than expected.

This sales information is also shared with distribution centers, as well as with vendors, through **electronic data interchange (EDI)**, that is, computer-to-computer exchange of business information in a structured format (Levy & Weitz, 2009). This information helps control inventory; for instance, if a store's inventory level of a specific product category drops below a predetermined level, the distribution center will automatically ship the products to the store. The shipment information is sent to the company's computer system so that the buyer or merchandiser knows the inventory levels in the store and distribution center. If the inventory level of the distribution center drops below a specified level, the buyer or merchandiser contacts the manufacturer to negotiate terms and shipping dates and to reorder merchandise. Using EDI and using POS data, executives can reduce the amount of time from order to delivery and decrease stock-outs (Levy & Weitz, 2009). Thus,

POS data help executives plan and control inventory levels and sales and respond quickly to fast-changing fashion trends.

Data mining tracks a variety of consumer and transaction information and identifies the relationships among factors using statistical techniques. Thus, data mining can be used in decision making and forecasting (Brannon, 2010). Once POS data are captured, the transaction information is stored in a company's database, known as a **data warehouse.** The data warehouse is the aggregation of all consumer information, including customers' shopping behaviors and demographics, sales history, promotions, and pricing. Apparel retailers and manufacturers have enormous information in their data systems (Brannon, 2010). The data stored in the data warehouse can be accessed at various levels and dimensions. As shown in Figure 4.3, data can be accessed according to the level of merchandise category (sales of t-shirt category), vendor (sales of Polo Ralph Lauren), and SKU (sales of Polo Ralph Lauren white t-shirts, size small). These data can also be accessed for different levels of the company—store (sales for a specific store in New York), division (sales for women's wear), or total company (total sales for the corporation). Finally, data can be accessed by point in time—day (sales for a specific day), season (sales for a specific season), or year (sales for a specific year). Thus, a data warehouse allows professionals within a company to access data on a number of different dimensions. For example, a CEO may be interested in quarterly or annual sales for a merchandise division, or a buyer might be interested in the sales for a specific vendor or day (Levy & Weitz, 2009). Data mining helps companies learn about customers' purchasing habits, gain insight into their preferences, establish marketing strategies, and predict future sales (Brannon, 2010).

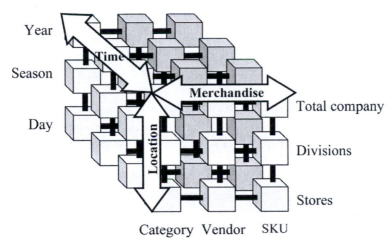

Figure 4.3 A data warehouse allows retailers and manufacturers to access POS information in various areas.

Source: Adapted from Levy, M., & Weitz, B. A. (2009). *Retailing management.* (7th ed.). New York: McGraw-Hill, p. 284.

Promoters are "professionals who emphasize and enhance an aesthetic product's value through verbal communication and/or design of the environment supporting the product or the brand" (Fiore, 2010, p. 17). Promoters advance a trend by trying to push the trend along the fashion curve, increasing its awareness and observability. These professionals are paid to promote particular products. For instance, advertisers are paid to develop an advertising campaign, which can persuade consumers to buy particular products. Other promoters in the fashion industry include fashion photographers, fashion show coordinators, marketing specialists, package designers, stylists, brand representatives, and visual merchandisers (Fiore, 2010).

Advertisers, stylists, and visual merchandisers as promoters in the fashion industry

Advertisers, or advertising agencies, provide services related to promoting products, using various channels, such as TV, radio, or billboards. Advertising, including TV commercials and billboards, increases the observability and familiarity of a brand or product, facilitating a consumer's innovation adoption process, as discussed in chapter 2. For example, DKNY was famous for its massive, iconic billboard in the trendy Soho neighborhood of New York City, which increased brand familiarity. Advertising can be used to promote trend colors or styles. For instance, in its TV commercials, Gap often shows models wearing a variety of colors to promote its new colors for the season, helping consumers become familiar with new trend colors so that they can easily adopt them. In 2005, the brand promoted feminine khakis as the season's hot item through its "Pretty Khaki" commercial. Thus, to develop creative ideas that fit the client's brand image or merchandise concept, it is essential for advertisers, particularly those dealing with fashion advertisements, to be familiar with trend forecasts.

To maintain a favorable image, companies or individuals (celebrities and politicians) often hire "creative" specialists, such as fashion stylists. Stylists may work as a company employee, agency employee, or freelancer (Stone, 2008). Fashion stylists select and coordinate apparel and accessories for store catalogs, print ads, Web sites, magazine articles, or commercials. Also, they may select fashion items for celebrity clients who influence the fashion adoption of end consumers. Stylists usually work with a team of other creative members, such as photographers, makeup artists, hairdressers, magazine editors, and the celebrity's agent or publicist (Stone, 2008). As shown in Case 4.1, forecasting materials are an important source for stylists to find the latest fashion information.

Visual merchandising is one of the most important activities that supports the selling of fashion merchandise (Stone, 2008). Visual merchandisers accentuate merchandise and illustrate concepts through the use of appropriate mannequins, lighting, colors, props, and signage. Well-executed visual merchandising attracts customers to the selling floor and encourages them to examine and try the merchandise and, therefore, increases sales. In addition to selling actual merchandise, visual merchandising can be used to introduce new products and fashion trends and to educate consumers about how the new apparel items can be worn and accessorized to complete the new look. Visual merchandisers continuously communicate with designers or buyers to discuss how merchandise should be displayed in a store or online. For instance, trend items and colors are usually displayed in the windows and other focal spots of a store. Thus, understanding the trends of the season is essential for visual merchandisers.

Forecasting as an integrated process

Figure 4.4 shows the general activities employed throughout the textile and apparel industry. It also illustrates the forecasting schedule, from initial color forecasting to yarn, textiles, and garment shows, as well as the production timeline for fibers, yarns, textiles, and apparel. Color forecasting agencies (e.g., CAUS and CMG) present new color trends nineteen to twenty-four months prior to the selling season. Other trend forecasting companies (e.g., The Doneger Group and WGSN) develop comprehensive trend forecasts for various markets (e.g., women's, men's, and/or youth/children's wear) twelve to eighteen months prior to the selling season. These trend forecasting organizations take into consideration the lead time required for fiber, yarn, and fabric producers and apparel manufacturers to produce their products, as well as the time required for retailers to order merchandise and have it in their stores at the right time.

Once determined, trend forecasts are used by a variety of professionals in the industry. First, trend colors are used by fiber and yarn manufacturers to compile their own color forecasts in the form of shade cards. Fiber and yarn manufacturers present new textile products along with the shade cards at yarn trade shows (e.g., Expofil and Pitti Immagine Filati), which are held ten and fifteen months before the selling season (Jackson, 2001). Fabric and knitwear companies then create their own colors in the development of fabrics or patterns based on both color forecasts from color organizations and from fiber and yarn company shade cards. The fabric products are presented in fabric shows (e.g., Premiere Vision), held eleven or twelve months ahead of the actual selling season.

Trend forecasts are also used by apparel manufacturers and retailers, which develop their merchandise a year in advance of the selling season. Often, designers or buyers are responsible for developing the color, fabric, and silhouette directions of their companies. They use trend forecasting materials to develop their interpretation of the trend for their market. Apparel designers and executives also visit fabric trade shows to look for inspiration, learn new trends, and find new sources, such as new fabric manufacturers and textile innovations. New apparel styles are presented in garment shows. Buyers visit these shows and/or vendors during the fashion weeks to buy merchandise, basing their choices on the fashion forecasts of their own brands or companies. They order merchandise two and six months before the selling season (Brannon, 2010).

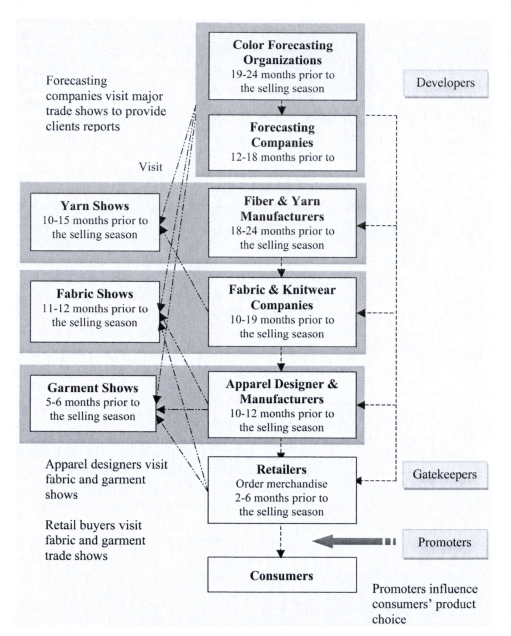

Forecasting companies visit major trade shows to provide clients reports

Color Forecasting Organizations
19-24 months prior to the selling season

Developers

Visit

Forecasting Companies
12-18 months prior to

Yarn Shows
10-15 months prior to the selling season

Fiber & Yarn Manufacturers
18-24 months prior to the selling season

Fabric Shows
11-12 months prior to the selling season

Fabric & Knitwear Companies
10-19 months prior to the selling season

Garment Shows
5-6 months prior to the selling season

Apparel Designer & Manufacturers
10-12 months prior to the selling season

Apparel designers visit fabric and garment shows

Retailers
Order merchandise 2-6 months prior to the selling season

Gatekeepers

Retail buyers visit fabric and garment trade shows

Promoters

Consumers

Promoters influence consumers' product choice

Figure 4.4 Forecasting is a team effort involving various professionals in the fashion industry.
Source: Developed by Hyejeong Kim.

Chapter Summary

- Fashion trend forecasting is developed by trend forecasting organizations or companies, merchandising and product development organizations, inspirational publications, and trade shows, all of which offer forecasting materials to retail clients.
- As developers, fashion forecasting companies develop their forecasting materials through the process of collecting information related to culture, the economy, politics, and technology, all of which influence future trends; conducting market and consumer research; and analyzing and synthesizing the information.
- Fashion trend forecasts are filtered and selected by gatekeepers (buying offices, retail buyers, and fashion magazine editors) who influence the styles and trends that will eventually be offered to consumers. Sales forecasting is an important process by which the new styles that will be introduced to consumers are selected.
- Selected by gatekeepers, new fashions are promoted by promoters (advertisers, Web sites, stylists, and visual merchandisers) who enhance the aesthetic value of the newly introduced products and increase consumer awareness.
- Fashion trend forecasting is developed, shared, and promoted by every sector and professional in the fashion industry and, thus, is an integrated process involving a team effort.

Key Terms

- Bloggers
- Color Marketing Group
- Consumer segmentation
- Competitive advantages
- Competitive Analysis
- Competitive environmental analysis
- Competitors
- Correlation and regression techniques
- Data mining
- Data warehouse
- Demographic segmentation
- Depth interviews
- Developers
- Editors
- Electronic data interchange
- Focus group interviews
- Gatekeepers
- Geographic segmentation
- Industrial espionage
- Lifestyle segmentation
- Market analysis
- Point-of-sales data
- Premiere Vision
- Projective technique
- Promoters
- Psychographic segmentation
- Qualitative research Quantitative research
- Retail buyers
- Sales forecasting
- Structured interview
- Stylesight
- Survey
- Sustainable competitive advantage
- The Color Association of the United States
- The Doneger Group
- Time-series
- Tobe Report
- Unstructured interview
- Worth Global Style Network

Questions for review and discussion

1. Select two or three trend forecasting companies in this chapter, and compare the services and types of trend information they provide clients. Discuss the differences and similarities.
2. Identify and discuss the sources and methods that fashion forecasters use to capture the signals of fashion change.
3. Compare different consumer research techniques, and discuss how each technique can be used by fashion companies. Provide some examples.
4. Identify some fashion brands or stores that target specific consumer geographic, demographic, geodemographic, or lifestyle segments. For instance, Harajuku Lovers, introduced in chapter 1, targets young consumers who like Japanese-inspired, cute products (lifestyle segment based on fashion preferences).
5. Identify the sources of sales forecasting, and discuss how each source can be used by fashion companies.
6. Identify promoters that are not mentioned in this chapter, and discuss their roles in the fashion industry.

Suggested Reading

McKelvey, K., & Munslow, J. (2008). *Fashion forecasting*. West Sussex, UK: Wiley-Blackwell.

References

Amit, R., Domowitz, I., & Fershtman, C. (1988). Thinking one step ahead: The use of conjectures in competitor analysis. *Strategic Management Journal, 9*, 431–442.

Blackwell, R. D., Miniard, P. W., & Engel, J. F. (2001). *Consumer behavior*. Troy, MO: Harcourt College Publishers.

Brannon, E. L. (2010). *Fashion forecasting* (3rd ed.). New York: Fairchild Books.

Brucker, L. (2010, May 3). In-depth with stylesight.com. [Web log comment]. Retrieved from http://fashionablymarketing.me/2010/05/in-depth-with-stylesight-com/

Burke, M . M. (2010, June). Following suit. *Vogue*, 88.

Churchill, G. A. Jr., & Iacobucci, D. (2005). *Marketing research: Methodological foundations*. Mason, OH: Thomson South-Western.

The Color Association of the United States. (n.d.). Retrieved from http://www.colorassociation.com/

Color Marketing Group. (n.d.). Retrieved from http://www.colormarketing.org/

Color trends and forecasting services. (n.d.). Retrieved from http://www.apparelsearch.com/Fashion/Forecasting/color_trends_forecasting.htm

Diamond, J., & Pintel, G. (2001). *Retail buying* (6th ed.). Upper Saddle River, NJ: Prentice Hall.

Diane, T., & Cassidy, T. (2005). *Colour forecasting*. Oxford: Blackwell Publishing.

Dickerson, K. (2002). *Inside the fashion business*. Upper Saddle River, NJ: Prentice Hall.

The Doneger Group. (n.d.). Retrieved from http://www.doneger.com/web/231.htm

Ferdows, K., Lewis, M. A., & Machuca, J. A. D. (2004, November). Rapid-fire fulfillment. *Harvard Business Review, 82*(11), 104–110.

Fiore, A. M. (2010). *Understanding aesthetics for the merchandising and design professional* (2nd ed.). New York: Fairchild Publications.

Fiore, A. M., & Kimle, P. A. (1997). *Understanding aesthetics for the merchandising and design profes-sional*. New York: Fairchild Publications.

Goodman, T. (2010, May). Rebel, rebel. *Vogue*, 187.

Gross, M. (1987, May 8). Women's Wear Daily and feuds in fashion. *The New York Times*, p. 20.

Holgate, M. (2010, March). Logged on. *Vogue*, 514.

Horyn, C. (1999, August 20). Breaking news with a provocative edge. *The New York Times*, p. 4.

Jackson, T. (2001). The process of fashion trend development leading to a season. In E. Hines & M. Bruce (Eds.), *Fashion marketing: Contemporary issue*. Jordan Hill, Oxford, UK: Butterworth Heinemann.

Jarnow, J., & Dickerson, K. G. (1997). *Insider the fashion business*. Upper Saddle River, NJ: Prentice Hall.

Jenkins, J. K. (2010, December). Market forces. *Vogue*, 188–190.

Lee, J. (2008, August 27). Gap. *Marketing*, 19.

Levy, M., & Weitz, B. A. (2009). *Retailing management* (7th ed.). New York: McGraw-Hill.

McKelvey, K., & Munslow, J. (2008). Fashion forecasting. West Sussex, UK: Wiley-Blackwell.

Miller, C. C. (2008, September 8). Designers of high fashion enter the age of high tech. *The New York Times*, p. 4.

Muller, C. S., & Smiley, E. L. (1995). *Marketing today's fashion* (3rd ed.). Englewood Cliffs, NJ: Prentice Hall.

Nolan, J. (2007). Sample competitive intelligence guidelines: Three level of complexity. Retrieved from http://www.ipo.org/AM/Template.cfm?Section=Search&section=Materials1&template=/CM/ContentDisplay.cfm&ContentFileID=55973

O'Brien, M. (2003, May 8). Ace of shades. *Late Edition*, 10.

Poulter, S. (2005, November 19). Cheaper fashions put the squeeze on Gap. *Daily Mail* (London), p. 57.

Premiere Vision. (n.d.). Retrieved from http://www.premierevision.fr/index.php?page=30&lang=en

Schiffman, L. G., Kanuk, L. L., & Wisenblit, J. (2010). *Consumer behavior*. Upper Saddle River, NJ: Prentice Hall.

Solomon, M. R., & Rabolt, N. J. (2009). *Consumer behavior in fashion*. Upper Saddle River, NJ: Pearson Prentice Hall.

Stone, E. (2008). *The dynamics of fashion* (3rd ed.). New York: Fairchild Publications.

Stylesight. (n.d.). Retrieved from http://www.stylesight.com/

Tay, M. (1998, September 2). Trend benders. *The Age* (Australia), 4.

Touliatos, J., & Compton, N. H. (1988). *Research methods in human ecology/home economics* (pp. 176–177). Ames, IA: Iowa State University Press.

Worth Global Style Network. (n.d.). Retrieved from http://www.wgsn.com/

5

CONSUMER AND INDUSTRY FASHION
INNOVATION AND DIFFUSION ACCELERATORS

Objectives

- Understand the factors that contribute to a style-confident consumer and his or her role in innovation adoption
- Understand the role of industry technology in accelerating product innovation and adoption
- Understand how consumer and industry trends may be used by firms to facilitate innovation adoption

The style-confident consumer

Changes in the consumer

As if fashion trend analysis and forecasting were not complex enough, fashion trends are changing more rapidly than ever before (Vejlgaard, 2008), thanks in part to changes in consumers and in the fashion industry. These changes have accelerated the rate at which an individual consumer goes through the five stages of consumer adoption of innovation (Beal, Rogers, & Bohlen, 1957). Part of the increase in speed of adoption is the result of consumers who are more confident in their personal style or taste.

Reflecting this more confident consumer is the rise of the **Creative Class,** which Richard Florida (2002) described as a growing economic class in which creativity is a key factor in professional roles. The Creative Class goes beyond designers, artists, writers, and musicians to include scholars, scientists, entrepreneurs, computer scientists, and engineers. Florida proposed that creativity is the driving force of economic growth. He estimated that 30 percent of the U.S. workforce and 25 percent to 30 percent of the workforce of industrialized European countries are classified as the Creative Class. This Creative sector accounts for one-half of all wages earned in the United States, which is more than is earned by manufacturing and service sectors combined. He stated that the Creative Class is causing a profound shift in the way people work, in values and desires, and in everyday lives. One of the changes is the increased value given to self-expression, individuality, and creativity, instead of conformity. This is manifested in the growing preference for products whose design innovations or uniqueness express individuality and creativity (Florida, 2002). The Creative Class has the desire and the money to buy innovations. Roberts (1998) echoed these ideas about the growing demand and disposable income of an expanding number of consumers who are looking for innovation in products and experiences. The financial resources of a growing number of consumers, combined with their desire for innovative products, may accelerate the development and diffusion of innovations. Designing products for and marketing products to this market segment may be an effective competitive advantage for a fashion firm.

Moreover, consumers in general no longer depend on quality to differentiate between products (Pine & Gilmore, 1999; Roberts, 1998). Instead, consumers use aesthetic (design) appeal to differentiate between products or brands. Consumers expect all products, from fashion apparel to flyswatters, to have an innovative design.

Industry responses to the style-confident consumer

Mass-market consumers expect high-price-point fashion innovations to diffuse quickly to lower price points (Figure 5.1). This helps drive product innovation—lower-price-point product designs change quickly to keep up with the changes in high-fashion designs, reinforcing rapid change among the latter as designers strive to keep their products unique. In Activity 5.1, explore some of the influences of high-price-point fashion innovations on lower-price-point trends. A growing number of retailers, including Carrefour, H&M, Kohl's, Target, and Wal-Mart, have now formed agreements with top fashion designers to bring an element of the designer's aesthetic to the mass market. Read Case 5.1, which illustrates how a top designer, Max Azria, will bring his aesthetic to Wal-Mart customers.

In support of this worldwide shift in consumer expectations, Postrel (2003) outlined the current **aesthetic imperative**, which stresses the importance of aesthetic appeal as consumers make decisions about their bodies, products, and environments. Making people, places, and things look good represents a growing segment of business (Penn, 2007; Postrel, 2003). For instance, consider the burgeoning growth in the number of cosmetic surgeons, nail salons, and tattoo parlors over the past fifteen years; you will recognize the increased interest in businesses catering to enhancing people's personal aesthetic appeal. Having a vast number of businesses that allow consumers to express the aesthetic imperative facilitates the development and diffusion of innovations. New businesses must recognize the importance of aesthetic appeal in their offerings to be competitive.

In terms of place, one visit to an American Girl Place, with its theater, café, and special events centered on its primary product (dolls), makes it clear that the shopping environment has come a long way from the old model of bland, never-ending shelves of products for purchase. Now, consumers expect **experiential marketing**

Figure 5.1 High-price-point fashion innovations (e.g., Phillip Lim's cape, on the left) diffuse quickly to lower price points (e.g., H&M's cape, on the right), driving further innovation.

Illustration source: Hui-Siang Tan.

CASE 5.1. MILEY CYRUS, MAX AZRIA SIGN DEAL WITH WAL-MART

Wal-Mart joins the ranks of other retailers, such as H&M, Target, and Kohl's, in offering a line of mass-designer apparel. Max Azria, designer of BCBG and CEO of Max Azria Group, has collaborated with teen idol Miley Cyrus (and her alter ego, Hannah Montana) to create a junior line for Wal-Mart called Miley Cyrus and Max Azria. The line includes tops, graphic T-shirts, pants, and shoes, priced under $20.

Cyrus is no stranger to Azria's designs. She donned a short Hervé Léger by Max Azria dress to the U.K. premiere of "Hannah Montana: The Movie." She wore a custom Hervé Léger by Max Azria black gown to the 2009 Grammy Awards. Cyrus will wear BCBG Max Azria styles when she tours for her album, and the tour will reportedly be sponsored by Wal-Mart.

The Wal-Mart project is Max Azria's second mass-market venture. His first was with France-based Carrefour. These agreements distinguish him because they are with two of the world's largest retailers—Wal-Mart and Carrefour. Azria designed a women's ready-to-wear collection for the French retailer, which operates hypermarkets in France, as well as Belgium, Brazil, China, Columbia [sic], Greece, Italy, Portugal, and Spain. The collection, called Tex, launched for the fall-winter 2007 season.

The BCBG Max Azria Group is a diversified organization with a portfolio of 22 brands, including BCBGeneration, Max and Cleo, and Manoukian. The price points range from $3,000 for a Hervé Léger dress at Bergdorf Goodman to a low of less than $20 for Miley Cyrus and Max Azria at Wal-Mart. Whereas Azria has some experience working with large retailers, industry observers said, "The difference with the line now [Miley Cyrus and Max Azria] is that this is truly a junior line" and that it was designed with a celebrity, Cyrus. Therefore, the collection bears both their names. This collection continues Wal-Mart's recent mining of popular culture as it relates to teens and has contributed to the discounter being able to consistently outpace its competition.

Source

Excerpts from Edelson, S. (2009, June 3). Miley Cyrus, Max Azria sign deal with Wal-Mart. *Women's Wear Daily*. Retrieved from http://www.wwd.com/retail-news/miley-cyrus-max-azria-sign-deal-with-wal-mart-2155427?src=rss/retail/20090603

ACTIVITY 5.1. FINDING FASHION INFLUENCES

Figure 5.1 provides an example of how product innovations quickly spread from one price point to another. Although the products are not identical, the influence of one design on the other is evident. Look at products found on low- and moderate-price-point retailers' Web sites, such as those of Target, Kohl's, or Macy's. Examine products from high-price-point fashion designers within the same season and see if you can identify the inspiration, similar to what was done in Figure 5.1. Place the low-, moderate-, and high-price-point product images next to one another in a Microsoft Word file, and explain what high-price-point design features were used as inspiration for the low- and moderate-price-point designs. Each student should collect at least three product similarities.

or retailing. This requires well-designed, engaging environments that offer unified brand *experiences*, interactions with informative brand representatives, and hands-on experiences with the new product. The end result is a consumer who has the knowledge she needs to confidently make purchase decisions.

From the firm's standpoint, new avenues of product trial may be necessary to keep pace with products' shortened product life cycle. Marketers "will have to find faster ways to build consumer awareness and trial of their new products since the lifespan of some new products will be as short as one year" (Roberts, 1998, p. 99). One form of experiential marketing is **pop-up retail**, which consists of stores and events that open for a limited time (Figure 5.2). For instance, Target, the master of pop-up retail, has opened pop-up stores for a short period in New York and London during their respective fashion weeks to showcase exclusive fashion products ("McQ," 2009). The eight-hundred-square-foot Colette x GAP pop-up store in New York City drew in many young consumers with its special products, which were exclusive to both the store and Colette in Paris, all jammed into the small space. As expected, a few items were sold out within the first hour of the opening ("Colette," 2008).

Pop-up retail depends heavily on word of mouth or on nontraditional advertising outlets, which adds to its appeal for consumers who like innovativeness and

Figure 5.2 Camel Active, a German men's sportswear brand, opened a pop-up store in an outdoor corridor of a Wuhan, China, shopping area.
Source: Ann Marie Fiore.

enjoy shopping (Kim, Fiore, Niehm, & Jeong, 2009). Not only do fashion change agents purchase the exclusive products offered in the temporary store, but also they provide positive word of mouth about the pop-up store experience and products, which may accelerate the adoption process among mainstream consumers. Creating experiential marketing venues may be just as important as the product design to the innovation's success; firms should create venues that not only inform the consumer but also create a positive "buzz" because of their excitement and uniqueness (Niehm, Fiore, Jeong, & Kim, 2007).

The consumer is surrounded not only by abundant physical examples of people, places, and things that emphasize aesthetics but also by media sources with copious design information (Vejlgaard, 2008), including TV programs such as *What Not to Wear*. Design and trend-related publications, Web sites, and "**ezines**" (online magazines) have grown in number. Complete collections from current international fashion shows and trend information can be found on numerous sites such as elle. com, style.com, and fashion.net. On fashion.net, consumers can sign up for trend newsletters from various sources, including Paris's trendsetting Colette shop and the bilingual dresslab.com. Some sources have begun to target a narrower group of consumers; for example, there are ezines that focus on the goth look (goth-style-secrets.com), runway fashion for the budget conscious (stylehog.com), or lifestyle for homosexual men (hesaidmag.com) (Figure 5.3). Having access to vast amounts

Figure 5.3 Targeted ezine hesaidmag.com provides design information, including apparel and interior design trends, to homosexual men.
Source: HeSaidMag.com.

of design and trend information enhances consumers' confidence as they make fashion decisions, which accelerates adoption of an innovation.

Exposure to design examples, information, and experimentation at every turn has led to a **style-confident consumer**. These are consumers who do not depend on an arbiter of taste to dictate how they or their environments should look. Instead, consumers of developed countries tend to be confident in their design preferences and engage in a **pluralistic aesthetic**, where personal style is determined by the individual, resulting in an array of simultaneously expressed styles accepted by the culture (Postrel, 2003). This pluralistic aesthetic helps drive innovation, but, at the same time, it creates a challenge for fashion forecasters because there is no single clear trend; instead simultaneous trends occur and should be acknowledged.

The role of industry technology in accelerating product innovation and diffusion

A partnership is a mutually beneficial relationship that involves sharing an undertaking, activity, or goal. Digital technology has facilitated partnerships between businesses. For example, digital technology that delivers in-store SKU-level sales information to manufacturers helps them reduce cash-flow-draining excess inventory and manage their production facilities more efficiently, while ensuring that products are replenished in the store to meet consumer demand (Lee, Pak, & Lee, 2003; Raftery, 2009). This leads to more profitable operations for both the manufacturer and the retailer and ushers the diffusion of new products. See Case 5.2, which provides an example of the use of Product Lifestyle Management (PLM) technology to facilitate a partnership between product developers and supplies to rapidly respond to consumer trends, accelerating delivery of fashion trends to consumers.

CASE 5.2. INDIA'S TRENT SELECTS ENOVIA APPAREL ACCELERATOR

Dassault Systemes announced today at the Prime Source Forum in Hong Kong that Trent Ltd., operator of Trent Westside, one of India's largest and fastest growing retailers, will use the ENOVIA Apparel Accelerator™ for Design & Development.

"As a market leader, it is imperative that we are able to stay ahead of the latest consumer trends. Our ability to understand what's happening at the point of sale and then effectively work with our suppliers and partners to translate this into new designs for subsequent seasons is crucial to our long term success," said Gaurav Mahajan, Head of Buying at Trent Ltd. "Based on our initial experience with ENOVIA V6 we have been impressed by Dassault Systemes ability to quickly deploy a PLM solution that provides us with greater visibility into the supply chain and an ability to track and manage costs and changes as necessary."

With 38 Westside stores in India and plans to expand rapidly in 2010, Trent Ltd. has to ensure that it can manage its margin and profitability by rapidly responding to changing market conditions and consumer trends. A key element of its long-term success will be based on how effectively the company is able to work with the core elements in their ecosystem including internal resources, partners, buyers, sourcing offices and suppliers. The ENOVIA Accelerator, which will take just nine weeks to implement, will integrate with their existing ERP systems to provide Trent Ltd. with greater visibility into the new product development process. This approach will enable the company to reduce sample development time and increase seasonal options by leveraging the market knowledge and design capabilities of key suppliers while also tracking commodity prices to negotiate better costs with them.

"In order to seize new opportunities and stay ahead of competition, retailers and apparel companies are starting to address the need for a more comprehensive approach to working collaboratively with their key suppliers. There's no doubt that the Indian RFA industry is extremely ambitious and companies are looking for the opportunity to expand into new markets. They understand that, as part of the process, sustainable and cost-efficient business can only be achieved by managing the product lifecycle from sample development to quality control," said Suman Bose, Country Director, Dassault Systemes India, Dassault Systemes. "We are pleased that Trent Ltd., a leader in the Indian retail market, has selected our solution as a key element to managing their long term success."

In addition to Westside, which was founded in 1998, Trent Ltd. also established Star India Bazaar in 2004, a chain of hypermarkets with stores in Ahmedabad, Mumbai and Bangalore. In 2005 Trent Ltd. rounded out its portfolio of brands with the acquisition of Landmark, India's largest book and music retailer.

The ENOVIA Apparel Accelerator™ for Design & Development is based on the Dassault Systemes V6 platform, a single PLM platform for managing product lifecycle business processes that will enable customers to implement industry standards and best practices. Designed as an out-of-the box solution, the Apparel Accelerator enables companies to rapidly deploy a state of the art, scalable enterprise solution for apparel design and development that can help them go to market quicker by taking products from trend to design to sourcing to manufacturing to the customer within a single, collaborative environment.

About Dassault Systemes

As a world leader in 3D and Product Lifecycle Management (PLM) solutions, Dassault Systemes brings value to more than 100,000 customers in 80 countries. A pioneer in the 3D software market since 1981, Dassault Systemes develops and markets PLM application software and services that support industrial processes and provide a 3D vision of the entire lifecycle of products from conception to maintenance to recycling. The Dassault Systemes portfolio consists of CATIA for designing the virtual product — SolidWorks for 3D mechanical design—DELMIA for virtual production—SIMULIA for virtual testing—ENOVIA for global collaborative lifecycle management, and 3DVIA for online 3D lifelike experiences.

Sources

Dassault Systèmes ENOVIA; INDIA: Leading Indian retailer to deploy Dassault ENOVIA Apparel Accelerator for Design & Development (2009, March 31). *Just-style*. Retrieved from http://www.3ds.com/company/news-media/press-releases-detail/release/leading-indian-retailer-trent-ltd-selects-dassault/single/2001/?cHash=b078740230f44f198 215352443007e30

Beal et al.'s (1957) model of innovation adoption (see chapter 2) was based on assumptions of one-way communication from a firm to consumers or two-way communication between consumers. Digital technology changes these assumptions because of the rise of multipath communication—consumers communicate back to the firm and among themselves simultaneously. This technology has facilitated the creation of strong, reciprocal relationships between businesses and consumers (Siwicki, 2006) and among consumers, which have accelerated product innovation and diffusion. Moreover, Beal et al.'s model does not capture the new partnership that consumers have with firms, that of innovation co-creator. Consumers no longer simply adopt what others have created; they now have a hand in the creation of the innovation. To remain competitive, firms should consider ways to harness the power of the consumer in the process of creating innovations.

The role of industry technology in accelerating consumer-inspired product innovation

Digital technology applications, including mass customization, "customer-made" practices, and rich media allow the consumer to become the co-creator of innovations. Through these applications, the innovation is shaped by the consumer; no longer does the consumer simply respond to the innovation offered by the firm. In addition, the product innovation becomes personalized and may not be diffused by the firm to other consumers.

Mass customization

One source of personalized product innovation for consumers is mass customization. **Mass customization** is a hybrid of mass production and customization and is defined as "the mass production of individually customized goods and services" (Pine, 1993, p. 48). Mass customization permits customer involvement in both the design process and the manufacturing processes (Duray, Ward, Milligan, & Berry, 2000).

Presently, mass customization is not a widely available option for many apparel and footwear firms because of its high cost, but some, including Ann Taylor, Lands' End, Timberland, and Nike in the United States, as well as Anna Ruohonen, Selve, and Rivolta in Europe (Piller, 2009), have employed mass customization. Smaller firms such as t-shirts.com, timbuk2.com, www.Zazzle.de, and 99dogs.com also provide mass customization of an array of products from t-shirts, computer bags, and lip balm.

One variation of mass customization involves **co-design**, in which a product's design is based on the consumer's selections from a range of design feature offerings. In co-design, the customer, generally with the aid of computer-assisted design (CAD) technology and/or professional assistance, creates an individualized product design from a company's style, fabric, color, surface design, and size alternatives (Figure 5.4). As an example of mass customization, Timberland allows a consumer to select from design options, including base, sole, stitching, and lace color, to create an individually designed shoe. Here, the innovation and evaluation processes are simultaneous. The consumer evaluates the innovation as it takes shape before his or her eyes. Then the product is manufactured for and shipped to the customer. Because the actual product is not present at the time of purchase, trial and adoption take place after receiving the product.

If fashion innovators use mass customization to create a unique product, it would be disadvantageous for the firm to destroy its uniqueness by mass-producing the design. Thus, individual co-designed innovations may not progress through the consumer adopter categories (e.g., early adopter, early majority), as mass-produced products generally do.

Crowdsourcing

Mass customization is different from the newer crowdsourcing movement ("Customer-made," 2006). Crowdsourcing is not consumer feedback commonly given to a company, nor is it mass customization, which occurs after companies have

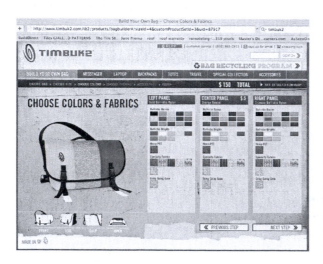

Figure 5.4 Timbuk2 allows consumers to mass-customize their bag by selecting from size, style, fabric color, and surface design options for the component parts.
Source: Jennifer Carroll, Timbuk2 marketing director.

decided which product options they will allow consumers to modify. Crowdsourcing, previously called **customer-made,** is "the phenomenon of corporations creating goods, services and experiences in close cooperation with experienced and creative consumers, tapping into their intellectual capital, and in exchange giving them a direct say in (and rewarding them for) what actually gets produced, manufactured, developed, [and] designed" ("Customer-made," 2006). The end result of a customer-made process may be totally new designs or modifications to current products, such as the new flavors, colors, flavor names, and graphics created in the Mountain Dew DEWmocracy 2 campaign. The innovative products are readied for mass production and undergo the collective diffusion process, starting with innovators and ending with late adopters, which further differentiates crowdsourcing from mass customization.

Although crowdsourcing is not a major trend at present for developing fashion innovations, a number of smaller firms are harnessing the creativity of consumers to develop designs for their product lines. For instance, threadless.com and the French version, lafraise.com, hold ongoing design competitions where consumers submit t-shirt designs, which are scored online for seven days. The winning designs are made available for sale. Shoe designer John Fluevog has a section on his fluevog.com site entitled "Open Source Footwear," where Fluevog owners can submit designs for future shoes or parts of shoes that will actually be put into production. Another small company, nakedandangry.com, incorporates crowdsourcing surface designs into its handbags, purses, dishware, men's ties, umbrellas, and wallpaper product lines. Site visitors score designs contributed to the nakedandangry.com site, and the high-scoring designs become part of the firm's catalog of product offerings. Thus, the consumer evaluation process for the innovation begins before the actual product is put into production. Moreover, the consumer doing this evaluation may not continue the innovation adoption process once the product in commercially available.

Businesses and consumers may benefit from crowdsourcing. Consumers are more inclined to persuade their friends and family to purchase a product they helped create, leading to powerful word of mouth for the firm (Cooper, 2010). In addition, the firm acquires product innovation input with minimal payment to the contributor, who may be awarded products, small cash awards, or a small portion of the profits from the new product ("Customer-made," 2006). For example, along with publishing the creator's name with the design, nakedandangry.com awards $750 and a product of the winner's choice from the site to the design contributor, making crowdsourcing a viable way of continually innovating the product line for smaller firms that cannot retain a large R&D or design team. "In an almost ironic twist, crowdsourcing is turning out to be a great vehicle for finding employment, as it helps companies recruit their next in-house designer, guerrilla advertising agency or brilliant strategist" ("Customer-made," 2006).

Because consumers have direct input into the product design and development process, customer-centric practices such as crowdsourcing innovations may have a better chance at success (Dziersk, 2009). Furthermore, the two-way communication found in mass customization and crowdsourcing processes may strengthen the relationship between the firm and the consumer. Higher satisfaction with the product and strengthened relationships may contribute to customer loyalty (Shankar, Smith, & Rangaswamy, 2002).

Although crowdsourcing may be a way to keep the product fresh without employing a large team of designers, it raises the question of the future role of designers. Designers may be employed to evaluate, enhance, and perfect designs, rather than originate them. For production, it may mean that more flexibility and short runs, perhaps using digital printers, will become necessary. The manufacturer will have to depend on quick response to get needed color pigments and dyes from the vender because the product line will not have been determined before the start of the new season.

In addition, the crowdsourcing trend is altering the expectations of consumers. Once they become accustomed to crowdsourcing, they will take even less kindly to corporations that don't communicate, don't respond to feedback, don't act upon suggestions, and keep pushing out new products in the hope that consumers will like them. Crowdsourcing is seen as a growing trend for the future:

> Customer-made may turn out to be one of the most exciting and long term engines behind change and innovation that the world of business has seen in years: a way of thinking that has the power to redefine the relationship between customer and brand, between consumer and producer, something that taps into the most awesome reservoir of intellectual capital ever assembled. ("Customer-made," 2006)

Rich media

Consumers can feel as if they are creating a personalized product combination of already manufactured products through the use of rich media. **Rich media** consists of Web site features that enable creation and manipulation of product *images* to simulate (or surpass) actual experience with the product(s). More than half of online consumers expect rich media and broadband applications (Demery, 2006). Vendaria, a company that develops rich media projects for retailers including JC-Penney and Wal-Mart, reported that incorporating rich media resulted in a 10 percent to 50 percent increase in online sales conversions (Demery, 2003). Rich media enhances consumers' attitude toward and willingness to purchase from, talk about, and return to the retail site (Fiore, Jin, & Kim, 2004; Fiore, Kim, & Lee, 2005; Lee, Fiore, & Kim, 2006; Shields, 2010), which supports the positive role of rich media in the adoption process.

Some examples of rich media include zoom features, mix-and-match product features, and more advanced rich media, termed "**virtual models**" (Figure 5.5), which allow the consumer to try product images on a virtual body form similar to his or her own. Apparel Web sites including Adidas, Home Shopping Network, H&M, Kenneth Cole, Lands' End, Lane Bryant, Sears, and Speedo, have incorporated mix-and-match and virtual model features. Incorporation of rich media has had a positive impact on product adoption in general. For instance, consumers who use My Virtual Model® (MVM) are 26 percent more likely to purchase, and they spend 13 percent more than those who do not use this feature on a site (Nantel, 2004). The updated Sears site, using this new technology:

> will allow consumers to virtually "try on" selected items using a personalized model of themselves to ensure that the style, color, pattern and fit are right before purchasing. . . . Shoppers can create countless combinations using a virtual model they can build and personalize to match their measurements—height, weight, body shape—and a headshot photo to ensure that the style, color, pattern and fit are right. . . . Shoppers can also email images of their looks to friends and family to help them make final purchasing decisions. ("Sears Transforms," 2008)

This suggests that rich media features may facilitate not only creation of fashion innovations through facile experimentation with new product combinations but also evaluation and trial stages of the adoption process during online shopping. The consumer can emulate the in-store shopping experience of trying the product on his or her body form and seeing the combination from a variety of angles, which may actually be more than what is possible in some fitting rooms. The consumer is not limited by exhaustion from trying innumerable product combinations. Instead of schlepping reluctant friends and family members along for their evaluation, customers can easily acquire their input via digital technology.

Future applications may want to allow the trial of new product combinations from a variety of retailers to further facilitate the evaluation and trial stages of adoption ("Style Avatars," 2008). In addition, more sites that resemble the multilingual stardoll.com and zwinky.com may incorporate entertainment elements (e.g., contests, games, chat, videos) with the practical elements of rich media to attract teen shoppers, who inadvertently become marketers for the brands when

Figure 5.5 *My Virtual Model™ provides rich media that allow a consumer to try products from various fashion brands on a personalized model.*

Source: Courtesy of My Virtual Model™.

they post avatars wearing fashion products. Allowing teens to share their personal style through dressed-up avatars may allow innovators to spark trends within this consumer group.

It may be worth the cost to include rich media in online marketing of a product innovation in order to facilitate not only the evaluation stage but also the adoption stage (when consumers keep and use the product). Moreover, firms may derive production and design innovation benefits from rich media:

- By capturing information about what details consumers zoom in on, the developer has a better sense of what influenced the consumers' purchases—what helped sell or detracted from the sale of the product or what costly detail was ignored.
- The combinations of products created by the consumer using rich media can give the developer a better sense of the aesthetic preferences of its customers and can spark ideas for future innovative designs and product assortments.
- Capturing consumers' body measurements as entered into the computer to create the virtual model gives developers a better sense of the relationship between its sizing standards and actual customers' measurements. This information may help the developer include or avoid design lines and details in an effort to enhance appearance of the product on the body.

Digital technology accelerating opinion leadership and innovation diffusion

Consumers are more than shoppers. They are digital content creators who exercise opinion leadership, which means they are a source of information that facilitates the innovation adoption process of others. A growing number of consumers use technology to create content about products and brands. For decades, consumers have been saving up their insights and complaints about the products they consume, simply because there were no adequate way to interact with companies or with other consumers. This is no longer true. "These [consumers] now can use hardware, software, and online distribution channels to share their insights and complaints easily with companies and other consumers globally" ("Customer-made," 2006). Content creators disseminate information through blogs, social networking sites (e.g., myspace.com, facebook.com, and twitter.com), unauthorized Web sites, and product reviews and product commercials for retail sites.

A growing number of consumers are looking to their peers rather than traditional advertising sources for product information and advice. This information and advice is taken seriously by consumers and can affect the evaluation stage of adoption for an innovation; it is the number one aid in consumer buying decisions cited by 91 percent of respondents in an e-tailing consumer survey (Wagner, 2006). Such consumer-created product information and advice can come from **blogs** (Figure 5.6), which are Web sites or parts of sites that contain ongoing commentary on products or topics contributed by a recognized or self-proclaimed expert(s), rather than by advertisers. Sites such as thisnext.com allow anyone to blog about his or her favorite fashion products. Some of the big-name fashion bloggers are Bryanboy, Mary Tomer,

Tommy Ton, Michelle Phan, and Yvan Rodic (Bryna, 2010). The fashion industry recognizes the power of bloggers to influence consumer opinion; some are now receiving front-row seat invitations to fashion week shows. There are blogs on general fashion and others on specific fashion product categories, including handbags, shoes, denim garments, and t-shirts. (see http://www.apparelsearch.com/Fashion/Fashion_Blogs.htm for a list of blogs on various fashion product categories and topics.) Try creating your own fashion blog in Activity 5.2.

Whereas blogs focus on an innovation, product category, or general topic, unauthorized Web sites focus on one firm or brand. These Web sites provide a place for detractors or admirers to gather, chastise, or praise a particular company/brand and keep up on the latest product or brand news. Product reviews may be as simple as content typed on a Web link, but many consumers have honed skills to create their own product commercials, facilitated by readily available and easy-to-master hardware and software. These product commercials, while not authorized by the

Daily Dose of Style   *September 14, 2011*

We can thank the inspiration of Indian design for many of the richly embellished styles we see right now. I have done my share of singing the praises of the great collection of embellished graphic T-shirts and sequined tanks offered by Express. Another Indian inspired winner is the Anarkali Kameez, which is a top or dress inspired by the legendary figure, Anarkali from Lahore (now part of Pakistan). Prince Saleem and Anarkali's story has parallels with the tragedy of *Romeo and Juliet*. The Anarkali Kameez is versatile, worn as a top with leggings and flats or as a dress with thigh-high boots. Colors and fabric vary from simple to sensuous. No need for jewelry; the trim at the neck and wrists does the trick. Try http://www.kaneesha.com

Anarkali Kameez tops

Figure 5.6 A blog provides ongoing commentary on products by an expert, rather than by advertisers.

Sources: Ann Marie Fiore; image courtesy of Yoon Jung Park.

ACTIVITY 5.2. CREATE YOUR OWN FASHION BLOG

Blogs are a way of reporting trends and evaluations of fashion innovations. Review the blogs on http://www.apparelsearch.com/Fashion/Fashion_Blogs.htm. Then, as a class, develop content for a blog focusing on a particular product category. If the class is large, break up into smaller groups to cover blogs on different product categories (e.g., shoes, purses, cosmetics, fragrances, watches). Each group member should review fashion news sites and periodicals; manufacturer, brand, and designer sites; brand-sponsored social networking sites; and other nonblog sites to identify new trends to post on your group's blog. Also, collect information from other sources, such as fashion shows, stores, or "people on the street." Each member should develop at least two posts and include images of the product innovations or trends for that product category. These posts should be created as a Microsoft Word document if the students do not have Web page development skills.

company, have an impact because of their global distribution, which can be accelerated by YouTube. The readily available information about a wide range of product innovations enriches consumer knowledge and evaluation and facilitates movement through the stages of innovation adoption.

Consumer-created content will become the standard way that consumers interact with shopping sites ("Pin Point," n.d.; Wagner, 2006). Many retail Web sites now contain a social networking component to build a closer connection with the consumer and foster brand loyalty ("Pin Point," n.d.). Furthermore, a rapidly growing number of major retailers, fifty-nine out of one hundred surveyed in 2008, have Facebook accounts (Choi, 2009). In 2011, 72 percent of the top British retailers had a Facebook presence (Bryant, 2011), which suggests continued growth in the use of social media by retailers. Many of these brand-sponsored social networking accounts provide consumers (fans) with an additional outlet for unbiased product reviews. Consumers go to social networking sites to interact with likeminded individuals and brand representatives ("Pin Point," n.d.). Moreover, through brand-sponsored networking accounts, the consumer can receive a quick response to a question or learn about special offers, events, and the latest innovation of a brand. "Madewell, the clothing chain owned by J. Crew, uses Facebook to keep shoppers informed of in-store parties and events such as 'Denim After Dark'. The idea is to make people feel they're a part of the brand. It's where people get the first word on what we're doing" (Choi, 2009). Mark Dzeirsk, vice president of design at Brandimage-Desgrippes & Laga, advised that firms use social networking sites to uncover what people who are invested in its brand honestly think to derive an early understanding if the innovation is headed for success or failure (Ryan, 2009). These various forms of dialog accelerate the dissemination of information and build a sense of trust and connectedness among consumers and with the brand in the evaluation stage. This may facilitate diffusion of innovation among consumers.

Product developers can glean valuable consumer-created information in real time to assess the latest fashion trends, which may lower the risk of missing trends when creating new product concepts. Some firms test consumer response by conducting previews of an upcoming line or product innovation with a select group of loyal customers ("Pin Point," n.d.). Consumer-created content can be a source of inspiration for design innovations and information about design problems. For instance, in a product review for a new bamboo and hemp fiber product, developers can learn many things from the consumer, such as their response to the unappealing stiffness of the fabric, which may lead to the failure of the innovation. Through product commercials created by consumers, developers can glean information about the adoption stage or about how their customer actually uses or wears the product, which can provide insight into design features or product combinations to build into the next innovation. Examine how information can be used to innovate design in Activity 5.3.

ACTIVITY 5.3. IDENTIFYING TRENDS FROM CONSUMER PRODUCT REVIEWS

Developers can gain information about needed design changes and innovations from the comments made by consumers in product reviews. Select five products from the same product category (e.g., dresses, coats, luggage, outdoor umbrellas) on a retailer's Web site (e.g., target.com). Read the reviews, identify at least five design changes needed, and propose at least five innovations for the product category. For instance, if a consumer comments about the unappealing stiffness of the coat fabric, you might suggest using softer fabric. This comment may move the manufacturer to use a stable knitted fabric rather than a woven fabric for the coat. If a reviewer comments that all luggage looks the same, you can suggest innovations in the design of the identity tag, product shape, or textile fabrications.

However, as with any data, issues of validity must be considered. Are the reviews or product information truly unbiased, and what is the demographic makeup of the reviewers? One may not be sure of the number of raters on a site and how well raters represent the target market for the innovation. There is nothing to stop unscrupulous firm employees from posing as consumers and providing high ratings. A wise firm understands that consumers are savvy and that, once trust is broken, it is very hard to regain; broken trust can have a long-term negative impact on the firm. **Triangulation of data** should be performed, which means checking whether the information gained from the consumer-created content agrees with information from other firm-generated sources, such as customer surveys, focus groups, and analysis of merchandising data.

In conclusion, we have seen how current consumer and industry trends are accelerating the innovation adoption stages within individuals and how this is affecting the diffusion of innovation. Fashion firms should use their knowledge of these consumer and industry trends to create better innovation and entice the consumer.

Chapter Summary

- There are a number of factors fostering a more style-confident consumer, which may accelerate innovation adoption. The financial resources of the Creative Class, with its desire for innovative products, and the vast number of businesses that allow consumers to express their aesthetic preferences together facilitate the development and adoption of innovations. Furthermore, experiential retailing and access to vast amounts of design and trend information enhance a consumer's confidence as she makes fashion decisions, accelerating diffusion of innovation.
- Digital technology has an impact on the five stages of the consumer adoption process model; however, this model does not capture the new partnership that consumers have forged in the innovation process, that of innovation co-creator. Digital technology applications, including mass customization, crowdsourcing practices, and rich media, allow the consumer to become the co-creator of innovations. Because consumers have direct input into the product design and development process via mass customization and crowdsourcing, innovations may have a better chance at success, and the processes may strengthen relationships between the firm and consumers.
- Consumers are digital content creators who exercise opinion leadership and can become a source of information that facilitates the innovation adoption process. Consumer-created content accelerates the dissemination of information and builds a sense of trust and connectedness among consumers and between consumers and the brand. This may facilitate adoption of innovations. Consumer-created content can also be a source of inspiration for design innovations.

Key Terms

- Aesthetic imperative
- Blogs
- Co-design
- Creative Class
- Crowdsourcing
- Experiential marketing
- Ezines

- Mass customization
- Pluralistic aesthetic
- Pop-up retail
- Rich media
- Style-confident consumer
- Triangulation of data
- Virtual model

Questions for review and discussion

1. Consider the most recent new style that you purchased. What were some of the sources of information that influenced your acceptance of the style (e.g., product reviews, hearing what online friends say, seeing the style on famous people? Which of these do you feel you weigh heavily in the adoption of a new style?

2. Try the mass customization or virtual function on an apparel Web site, such as timberland. com, nike.com, or landsend.com. Discuss how the experience affected your evaluation and willingness to adopt the product. Did it enhance your confidence that you were selecting the right product?
3. Are there other examples of technology that have accelerated fashion diffusion?

Suggested Readings

Gogoi, P. (2007, February 9). Pop-up stores: All the rage. *Business Week*. Retrieved from http:// www.businessweek.com/bwdaily/dnflash/content/feb2007/db20070206_949107.htm

Roberts, S. (1998). *Harness the future*, chap. 5: "Technology" (pp. 85–105); chap. 10: "Consumer Psyche" (pp. 171–193). Toronto, Ontario: John Wiley & Sons.

Vejlgaard, H. (2008). *Anatomy of a trend*, Epilogue, "A continuing story: The future of trends" (pp. 193–202). New York: McGraw-Hill.

References

Beal, G. M., Rogers, E. M., & Bohlen, J. M. (1957). Validity of the concept of stages in the adoption process. *Rural Sociology, 22*(2), 166–168.

Bryant, M. (2011, April 8). Major UK retailers still surprisingly poor at social media engagement. *The Next Web*. Retrieved from http://thenextweb.com/uk/2011/04/08/major-uk-retailers-still-surprisingly-poor-at-social-media-engagement/

Bryna. (2010, February 22). Vogue March 2010: Logged on. *Mama's a Rolling Stone*. Retrieved from http://mamasarollingstone.com/vogue-march-2010-logged-on/

Choi, C. (2009, April 15). Make friendship pay: Get Twitter, Facebook deals. *Associated Press*. Retrieved from http://www.azcentral.com/business/consumer/articles/2009/04/15/20090415biz-OntheMoney0415.html

Colette x GAP-NYC pop-up store—opening day. (2008, September 8). *Freshnessmag*. Retrieved from http://www.freshnessmag.com/2008/09/08/colette-x-gap-nyc-pop-up-store-opening-day/

Cooper, F. (2010, May 24). Discussion of the week. *Forbes.com*. Retrieved from http://www.forbes.com/2010/05/24/frank-cooper-pepsico-consumer-engagement-cmo-network-discussion-of-the-week.html?feed=rss_leadership_cmonetwork

Customer-made. (2006, May). *Trendwatching.com*. Retrieved from http://www.trendwatching.com/trends/CUSTOMER-MADE.htm

Demery, P. (2003, October). The latest flash. *Internet Retailer* [online]. Retrieved from http://www.internetretailer.com/article.asp?id=10323.

Demery, P. (2006, January). As consumers flock to high bandwidth, e-retailers shake, rattle and roll. *Internet Retailer*, pp. 23–28.

Duray, R., Ward, P. T., Milligan, G. W., & Berry, W. L. (2000). Approaches to mass customization: Configurations and empirical validation. *Journal of Operations Management, 18*, 605–635.

Dziersk, M. (2009, June 1). Six ways to avoid landing in the product failure bin. *Fast Company*. Retrieved from http://www.fastcompany.com/blog/mark-dziersk/design-finds-you/6-ways-avoid-landing-product-failure-bin

Edelson, S. (2009, June 3). Miley Cyrus, Max Azria sign deal with Wal-Mart. *Women's Wear Daily*. Retrieved from http://www.wwd.com/retail-news/miley-cyrus-max-azria-sign-deal-with-wal-mart-2155427?src=rss/retail/20090603

Fiore, A. M., Jin, H. J., & Kim, J. (2004). For fun and profit: Image interactivity, hedonic value, and responses towards an online store. *Psychology & Marketing, 22*(8), 669–694.

Fiore, A. M., Kim, J., & Lee, H-H. (2005). Effects of image interactivity on approach responses towards an online retailer. *Journal of Interactive Marketing, 19*(3), 38–53.

Florida, R. (2002). *The rise of the creative class.* New York: Basic Books.

INDIA: Leading Indian retailer to deploy Dassault ENOVIA Apparel Accelerator for Design & Development. (2009, March 31). *Just-style.* Retrieved from http://www.3ds.com/company/news-media/press-releases-detail/release/leading-indian-retailer-trent-ltd-selects-dassault/single/2001/?cHash =b078740230f44f198215352443007e30

Kim, H-J., Fiore, A. M., Niehm, L., & Jeong, M. (2010). Creative Class consumers' behavioral intentions towards pop-up retail. *International Journal of Retailing and Distribution Management, 38*(2), 133–154.

Lee, H-H., Fiore, A. M., & Kim, J. (2006). Technology acceptance model, shopping orientation, image interactivity technology, and consumer responses toward an online retailer. *International Journal of Retail and Distribution Management, 34*(8), 621–644.

Lee, S. C., Pak, B. Y., & Lee, H. G. (2003). Business value of B2B electronic commerce: The critical role of inter-firm collaboration. *Electronic Commerce Research and Applications, 2,* 350–361.

McQ by Alexander McQueen for Target. (2009, February 15). *Liberty London Girl.* Retrieved from http://libertylondongirl.blogspot.com/2009/02/mcq-by-alexander-mcqueen-for-target.html

Nantel, J. (2004). My virtual model: Virtual reality comes into fashion. *Journal of Interactive Marketing, 18*(3), 73–86.

Niehm, L., Fiore, A. M., Jeong, M., & Kim, H-J. (2007). Pop-up retail's acceptability as an innovative business strategy and enhancer of the consumer shopping experience. *Journal of Shopping Center Research, 13*(2), 1–30.

Penn, M. J. (2007). *Microtrends: The small forces behind tomorrow's big trends.* New York: Hachette Book Group.

Piller, F. (2009, October 13). MCPC 2009 Conference Report Day 4: Fashion Lab: Anna Ruohonen, Selve, Servive, Rivolta on why customization is the true luxury in fashion. *Mass Customization & Open Innovation News.* Retrieved from http://mass-customization.blogs.com/mass_customization_open_i/clothing/

Pin Point. (n.d.). *PTC.* Retrieved from http://www.ptc.com/WCMS/files/84952/en/4050_Pin Point_VoiceUser_finalHR.pdf

Pine, B. J., II. (1993). *Mass customization.* Boston: Harvard Business School Press.

Pine, B. J., II, & Gilmore, J. H. (1999). *Experience economy: Work is theater and every business a stage.* Boston: Harvard Business School Press.

Postrel, V. (2003). *The substance of style.* New York: HarperCollins.

Raftery, D. (2009, June 8). Optimizing cash flow with SKU-level forecasting. *Retail Wire.* Retrieved from http://www.retailwire.com/Discussions/Sngl_Discussion.cfm/13791

Roberts, S. (1998). *Harness the future.* Toronto, Ontario: John Wiley & Sons.

Ryan, T. (2009, June 8). Tips for avoiding product failure. *Retail Wire.* Retrieved from http://www.retailwire.com/Discussions/Sngl_Discussion.cfm/13792

Sears transforms the online shopping experience with help from IBM and My Virtual Model. (2008, September 17). *Yahoo Finance.* Retrieved from http://biz.yahoo.com/iw/080917/0434799.html

Shankar, V., Smith, A. K., & Rangaswamy, A. (2002). *Customer satisfaction and loyalty in online and offline environments.* Working Paper from e-commerce MIT. Retrieved from http://e-commerce.mit.edu/papers/ERF/ERF218.pdf

Shields, M. (2010, March 17). Engagement is key for rich media video ads. *Brandweek*. Retrieved from http://login.vnuemedia.com/bw/content_display/news-and-features/digital/e3i81da 41243576aea0d081cb45b438bd2e

Siwicki, B. (2006, October). The view from the top. *Internet Retailer*, pp. 31–39.

Style avatars—H&M rocks online retail. (2008, November 12). *Digital Vinyl*. Retrieved from http://www.digitalvinyl.dk/?p=418

Vejlgaard, H. (2008). *Anatomy of a trend*. New York: McGraw-Hill.

Wagner, M. (2006, August). Clicking on all cylinders. *Internet Retailer*, pp. 23–28.

6

SOCIAL RESPONSIBILITY
AND SUSTAINABILITY RELATED
TO FASHION TRENDS AND FORECASTING

Objectives

- Understand the definitions of social responsibility and sustainability
- Understand the increase of waste caused by the rapid diffusion of innovations
- Understand the role of mass customization in slowing down consumers' desire for new fashion
- Understand the impacts of social responsibility and sustainability on fashion trends
- Understand the contribution of Internet information on socially responsible consumer decisions
- Understand firms' cost concerns regarding environmental improvements and programs to encourage socially responsible business practices

Definitions of social responsibility and sustainability

The previous chapter provides evidence that the speed of fashion trend diffusion is accelerating. This may result in more consumption and waste. The present chapter offers a counterargument—that consumers are becoming more aware of the social impact of their purchases and are looking to reduce (the impact of) their consumption. In response to the pressures of a rapidly growing world economy, social responsibility and sustainability have become increasingly important concepts that affect many aspects of the fashion business. Contemporary consumers are making consumption decisions that reflect their desire to protect the environment. Consequently, many companies have embraced a "green marketing" concept to capture the environmentally conscious market (Kim & Damhorst, 1998).

To begin our discussion, it is important to define the terms "**social responsibility**" and "**sustainability.**" In fact, there are many definitions of these two concepts in the current literature, and often they are used interchangeably. In fact, they have been defined differently in different fields. Carroll (1999) traced the evolution of the concept of social responsibility since the term's first appearance in the business literature of the 1950s. Specifically, economist Howard Bowen first used the term, defined broadly as the obligations of businesspeople to pursue policies, to make decisions, or to take actions that are desirable in terms of the objectives and values of our society (as cited in Carroll, 1999). In the 1960s, the concept was expanded to include the benefits of sustainability to society as a whole, and several large companies began to take emerging leadership roles (Dickson, Loker, & Eckman, 2009). During the 1980s and 1990s, a variety of terms were used interchangeably to describe social responsibility, such as "business ethics" and "sustainability" (Dickson & Eckman, 2006). The organization Business for Social Responsibility, whose goal was to help businesses achieve social responsibility, proposed that companies achieve commercial success in ways that honor ethical values and respect people, communities, and the natural environment and that they integrate socially conscious policies and practices into every aspect of their operations (Dickson, Loker, & Eckman, 2009).

Social responsibility is an umbrella term that covers all responsible practices related to labor standards, human rights, and the environment. Sustainability implies improving, building upon, and achieving responsible practices that are maintained over the long term (Dickson, Loker, & Eckman, 2009). According to Stern and Ander (2008), sustainability is defined as "a system utilizing renewable resources that meets the requirements of the present without compromising the requirements of future generations or disrupting present or future environmental balance" (p. 40). Dickson, Loker, and Eckman (2009) argued that sustainability is the ultimate goal of successful socially responsible practices, which improves the lives of people and the health of the environment for the future.

Until the 1990s, there was little discussion about the environmental impacts of the production and consumption of apparel or other products. During the previous decade, labor issues had received the most attention, but environmental issues then emerged as the next area of social responsibility that companies were expected to address (Dickson, Loker, & Eckman, 2009). Since that time, many companies have focused their efforts on the adoption of environmentally friendly materials and on production processes that reduce the use of toxic chemicals and cut **waste.** In addition, the importance of total energy use, including transportation costs for production and distribution as well as end-of-life options such as **recycling, redesign,** and **biodegradable** disposal, has been integrated into business strategies (Dickson, Loker, & Eckman, 2009). Companies such as Patagonia and Timberland moved quickly in this direction and began integrating both environmental stewardship and social responsibility into their mission, vision, and business strategies (Dickson, Loker, & Eckman, 2009). There are numerous other companies now focusing on sustainability, including Gap, Banana Republic, Nike, Liz Claiborne, Levi Strauss & Co., and Philips-Van Heusen.

Increased waste due to rapid diffusion of innovation

Change is an essential component of fashion, and the process of change inevitably produces waste (Kaiser, 2008). Moreover, with the advent of **fast-fashion** retailers, garments are increasingly more disposable. Some consumers buy new, inexpensive clothes every two weeks (Rosenthal, 2007). The European companies Zara and H&M, which created the notion of fast fashion, shortened the fashion cycle and accelerated the speed of retail (Stern & Ander, 2008). Although Zara is admired for its efficient and profitable fashion replenishment cycle, which delivers new product styles every two weeks, it unfortunately also promotes overconsumption by encouraging consumers to buy frequently (Dickson, Loker, & Eckman, 2009). Many of today's retailers no longer have four to five fashion collections per year; instead, new fashions arrive daily to retain consumer interest and stimulate sales (Frings, 2005).

In this era of fast, disposable fashion, both designers and consumers must consider the problem of postconsumer waste (Welters, 2008). Hawley (2006) argued that a sustainable fashion system could be viewed from a production-consumption perspective. She stated that a balanced system produces garments that match the rate of consumption and manages waste through reuse, recycling, and biodegradable approaches. U.S. current fashion system produces much more than consumers need, contributing excessive fabric and garment waste to **landfills** (Hawley, 2006). Kaiser (2008) argued that it is necessary to identify processes that can reduce or eliminate the consequences of overconsumption. Specifically, strategies must be implemented to reduce the production of unwanted product and to persuade consumers to buy fewer, higher-quality garments.

The role of mass customization in slowing down consumers' desire for new fashion

There are various methods available to slow down consumers' adoption of new fashion. One method is to make clothing items that are more durable and long-lasting so that they need not be replaced as frequently (Chen & Burns, 2006). However, making the right product is probably the best approach to achieving a sustainable fashion system. Thus, a custom fashion system that makes the right amount of the right product is very effective in achieving sustainability (Loker, 2008). The business strategy for producing and delivering the right product at the right time to the right place is **mass customization** (Pine, 1993). Mass customization combines the efficiency of mass production and the individualization of custom design. Clothing is made on-demand, only when there is a customer to buy it, and it is customized for style, size, or function with the assistance of technology. Technology involves consumers in the design and product development process so that the resulting product is exactly what the consumer wants. For example, body-scan technology improves fit, reducing the flow of apparel unsold and returned apparel because it fits poorly. Customization creates single, individualized products and facilitates a sustainable fashion system by decreasing the flow of product and waste in the system.

In addition to mass customization, digital textile printing, seamless knitting, made-to-order clothing, wearable technology, and smart fabrics are other technological innovations that reduce product waste by creating customized garments or enhancing function. Digital textile printing is used to print only ordered items; it enables producers to match production to consumption. Wearable technology and smart fabrics, which address personal needs by monitoring biological health, adjusting to temperature or moisture, and creating sound, add meaning to a garment for the wearer and extend a product's life span. These technology-enabled apparel applications allow for a future of design and product development that has abundant possibilities for developing sustainable solutions (Loker, 2008).

The influence of social responsibility and sustainability on fashion trends

Many sustainable movements and practices are gaining momentum and moving toward the mainstream of society. While green buildings, interiors, and home products flourish, fashion also holds a great potential impact on sustainability (Hethorn & Ulasewicz, 2009). **Sustainable design** refers to the practice of maintaining quality of life by using creative and innovative design ideas to substitute less harmful products and processes for conventional ones. Thus, sustainable design requires designers to think creatively and about possible strategies in the global apparel industry (Dickson, Loker, & Eckman, 2009). Now is the time fashion professionals should consider giving fashion design new directions and motivations in line with the sustainability movement, and designers may be a crucial component of the movement (Fletcher, 2008).

In order to determine its **environmental friendliness,** six distinct aspects of an apparel product's life cycle can be considered: product design, materials selection, production and sourcing, distribution (packaging and transportation), product care or maintenance, and end-of-use management (Dickson, Loker, & Eckman, 2009). First, creative garment design and pattern-making ideas that minimize fabric waste can reduce the environmental impact. Next, bio-based material selection, the selection of materials that are made from recyclable materials or that can be recycled and that are not processed or finished with toxic chemicals, can decrease harm to the environment (Sustainable Textile Standard, n.d.). Secondhand garments can also be recycled into new designs as another way to facilitate sustainability. A current example includes a line of high-priced ready-to-wear shirts, skirts, and dresses by Alabama Chanin that was created from used t-shirts that have been recut and embellished. Retailers have also begun to sell recycled collections, such as the Urban Renewal Collection by Urban Outfitters (Dickson, Loker, & Eckman, 2009). New concepts are still needed that rethink not only material components but also the process of garment design, production, use, disposal, and reuse (Hethorn & Ulasewicz, 2008).

Consumers continue to cite drawbacks related to sustainable garments. In addition to the fact that they may find the color or style of an organic garment not very stylish (e.g., they often use earth tones or off-white colors), the prices of organic and recycled textile products are often higher than those of regular items (Chen

& Burns, 2006; Ortega, 1994). To combat this issue, Wal-Mart and General Electric are promoting green products by bringing unit costs in line with those for the products' nongreen counterparts; it is now possible to buy an organic v-neck shirt at Wal-Mart for about the same price as one made from conventionally grown cotton (Laszlo, 2008). Mainstream suppliers such as Wal-Mart, General Electric, and DuPont are now promoting sustainability as part of their brand image or culture, which becomes a source of competitive advantage (Laszlo, 2008).

Companies in the United Kingdom have also made corporate social responsibility a high priority. For example, Marks & Spencer, the British retailer of clothing, food, and home products, has formally committed to corporate social responsibility (Stern & Ander, 2008). Marks & Spencer first published information on environmental issues in 1990. The company began publishing comprehensive reports on corporate social responsibility in 2003 with its "Corporate Social Responsibility Review." Since that time, the company has issued corporate social responsibility reports alongside its annual reports. In January 2008, the company announced Plan A, its five-year, one-hundred-point eco-plan to help sustain the environment (Stern & Ander, 2008).

The following section discusses the influence of sustainability and social responsibility on fashion trends, consumer trends toward green products, consumer trends against the use of real fur or leather, consumer trends toward recycled fashion, and **minimum-fabric-waste fashion** in design and product development.

Consumer trends toward green products

Dan Butler, vice president of merchandising and retail operations for the National Retail Federation, asserts, "**Green** is not a trend. It's a new way of life for us. Going green is not going to go away" (cited in Stern & Ander, 2008, p. 111). "Going green" has affected every aspect of our culture, and fashion is not immune to its influence. Greentailing—incorporating sustainability into retailing—is moving from concept to practice, connecting eco-conscious consumers and becoming a crucial element of the future of retail, although it is still early in the development cycle (Stern & Ander, 2008). "Green is the new black": this metaphor from Suzy Menkes, reporter for the *International Herald Tribune* (2006), creates a useful analogy between eco-friendliness and fashion that reflects the cultural mood of caring about the environment. This metaphor enables us to envision the possible connections among sustainability, profit (i.e., being in the black accounting wise), and fashionability (Kaiser, 2009). However, to achieve this synthesis, the fashion industry, which previously focused on aesthetics, must develop a new standard in defining fashion with a balance of environmental sensitivity and aesthetics (Baugh, 2008).

When consumers became increasingly aware of sustainability, in the 1990s, organic cotton, Sally Fox's naturally colored cottons (e.g., FoxFibre®), and **hemp** drew our attention (Welters, 2008). **Organic cotton** is an eco-friendly fiber because it uses lower amounts of insecticides and herbicides than are required for traditionally grown cotton. The use of organic cotton has expanded from bed sheets and towels to women's wear, baby clothes, and even teenage fashion. The market is increasing each year; in fact, retail sales of organic cotton have more than doubled in four years in the early 2000s (Laszlo, 2008). Figure 6.1 shows a 100 percent organic cotton collection created by Sanko. One example of the best use of organic cotton is the new product line of Eco2Cotton™. It requires no new water to grow; utilizes no fertilizers, no insecticides, and no dyes; and produces no waste (Ulasewicz, 2008b). In addition to organic cotton, green cotton that has been washed with mild, natural-based soap, is not bleached or treated with any chemicals, except possibly **natural dyes** (Kadolph, 2007).

Natural fibers are often associated with environmental responsibility, but this association is not necessarily correct, as fiber content alone may not be an accurate indicator (Chen & Burns, 2006). When comparing the "greenness" of cotton and polyester, the average consumer, for example, will assume that cotton is more environmentally responsible than synthetic polyester because cotton is a natural fiber. Although cotton is renewable and polyester is made from nonrenewable sources, the current conventional cotton production system is in fact heavily dependent on pesticides and fertilizers (Chen & Burns, 2006). Consumers are usually unaware of these environmental hazards and should become more educated about sustainable materials and products.

Figure 6.1 A 100 percent organic cotton collection created by Sanko.
Source: Eundeok Kim.

The main problems with synthetic polymers are that they are nondegradable and nonrenewable. Furthermore, the use of synthetic fibers has significantly increased the nation's oil consumption; oil and petroleum are nonrenewable resources, and, at the current rate of consumption, these fossil fuels are expected to last for only another fifty to sixty years (Blackburn, 2005). Of even more concern is the fact that polymeric fibers do not readily degrade, and, when disposed of, they increase the amount of waste in landfills, which are fast decreasing in number throughout the world. Several years ago, the Republic of Ireland declared that it no longer had any space for landfills and imposed large taxes on the use and disposal of polymers. Landfill space in the United Kingdom is also decreasing (Stevens, 2002).

The ecologically destructive fibers of cotton and polyester account for around 80 percent of the world fiber market (Blackburn, 2005). Therefore, a large majority of the textiles used in contemporary fashion are not sustainable. To replace these destructive materials, natural materials such as hemp and bamboo, biodegradable synthetics such as corn starch and soya bean fibers, and cellulose manufactured from sustainably harvested eucalyptus can be used ("How to recycle," 2009). From these raw materials, new fabrics can be created. Examples are Eco-Spun, a wool-like fabric made from recycled soda bottles; Lenpur, a cashmere-like fabric made from the wood pulp of white pine trees; soya, a silky and soft cotton-like fabric made from soybeans; and sasawashi, a naturally absorbent cotton- or linen-like fabric made from a mixture of kumazasa bamboo and washi (Ulasewicz, 2008a).

Of all the interesting new fibers, **bamboo** is one of the most favored by designers. Bamboo is a fast-growing grass and is pest-resistant ("China Bambro Textile Company," 2003). Its fibers have a soft hand, and it drapes well. It also combines well with other fibers, such as cotton, Lycra®, and silk (Ulasewicz, 2008a). In addition, it is easily dyed, producing beautiful colors not possible in cotton ("China Bambro Textile Company," 2003). Unfortunately, the hard outer core of bamboo must be broken down to make the fiber usable for spinning into yarn, and chemicals are required in this process. According to Oakes (2006), if bamboo is to be considered truly sustainable, scientists must first eliminate the need for chemicals in its processing (cited in Ulasewicz, 2008a).

Corn is also being used as an alternative dextrose source because of its abundance and low cost. Fabrics made from corn fiber seem to have the comfort and hand of natural fibers along with having the performance, cost, and easy care of synthetics (Kelly, 2003). Soya bean protein fibers create warm, soft, comfortable, wool-like fibers. Recent developments in creating biodegradable fibers from renewable resources have revived interest in these fibers (Blackburn, 2005).

In 2003, the first Ethical Fashion Show®, founded by Paris designer Isabelle Quéhé, was hosted in Paris. The annual European event features designers who use fibers and dye processes that support the environment. The styles presented at the show aim for a balance among creativity, quality, and price. Products are manufactured with raw materials and dyes that are not harmful to the environment (Ulasewicz, 2008a). In recent years, an increasing number of green fashion shows have been held in major fashion cities in the United States, such as New York and Chicago. In addition, a growing number of designers use organic materials to create stylish collections. Carol Young's boutique Undesigned is an example. Her clothing lines include textiles made from soy, bamboo, hemp, and organic cotton. Figure 6.2 shows an organic cotton fleece bolero and a linen top and skirt with silk trim for the SS 06 Collection created by Undesigned.

Swedish retailer H&M launched its first collection featuring 100 percent sustainable materials in March 2010. "The Garden Collection" represented a major step toward fulfilling H&M's promise to increase its use of organic products each year until it reaches 50 percent of all products sold, in 2013 ("H&M to launch," 2010). This collection, including floral prints and a 1970s flower-power design, was made using organic and sustainable materials such as organic cotton, organic linen, and recycled polyester made from PET-bottles and Tencel. Karolina Dubowicz, from H&M's Communication and Press Department, mentioned, "Promoting organic cotton is part of H&M's environmental strategy—we encourage cotton farmers to switch to organic cultivation. We also want to make it possible for our customers

Figure 6.2 An organic cotton fleece bolero and a linen top and skirt with silk trim for the SS 06 collection by Undesigned.
Source: Carol Young.

to make a greener choice, which is another reason we offer garments with certified organic cotton" ("H&M to launch," 2010). In this section, a variety of green products was discussed. As a further example, Case 6.1 illustrates a 100 percent organic cotton product by Gap.

CASE 6.1. GAP'S 100 PERCENT ORGANIC COTTON MEN'S T-SHIRTS NOT CHEMICALLY DYED

Gap Inc. began offering organic cotton t-shirts for men at more than 500 Gap stores in North America. The shirts were introduced in response to increasing customer demand and as part of the company's commitment to finding innovative, socially responsible ways to make its products. In order to preserve the natural colors and qualities of the organic cotton fiber, Gap's organic cotton t-shirts have not been bleached or chemically dyed. Each shirt has a hangtag indicating that it is made with "100 percent organic cotton." Certified organic cotton is grown without the use of synthetic pesticides or fertilizers that are harmful to the environment. The t-shirts are made in three different styles—v-neck, crewneck, and tank—and the retail price is $16.50. Kindley Walsh Lawlor, Senior Director of Strategic Planning and Environmental Affairs for Gap Inc., said, "Our customers have shown a real interest in responsibly produced products. . . . We're always exploring new ways to make our products, and we're excited to offer environmentally sensitive items we think our customers will love."

Gap is exploring more use of organic cotton, anticipating the introduction of additional items made with organic cotton in the next few seasons. These products made from sustainable fibers underscore the company's commitment to ethical sourcing. In 2005, the company joined the Better Cotton Initiative (BCI), a multi-stakeholder initiative with the goal of promoting more sustainable cotton cultivation practices worldwide. BCI encourages the adoption of better management practices in cotton cultivation to achieve measurable reductions in environmental impact while improving social and economic benefits for cotton farmers globally. Other members of the initiative include the International Communications Consultancy Organization (ICCO), Organic Exchange, World Wildlife Fund (WWF), and the United Nations Environmental Programme (UNEP) as well as other well-known brands and retailers.

Source

Gap Inc. (2007, March 20). Organic cotton t-shirt debut at Gap. *The Corporate Social Responsibility Newswire*. Retrieved from http://www.csrwire.com/press_releases/25693-Organic-Cotton-T-Shirts-Debut-at-Gap

---

Consumer trends against the use of real fur and leather

In the twentieth century, fur underwent a spectacular rise and fall, going from widespread popularity in the first half of the century to infamy in the second half, when it became the target of animal protection campaigns by environmentalists.

While high-profile campaigns in the 1990s caused consumers to doubt the moral legitimacy of wearing fur, in recent years, fur once again has gained popularity in the consumer market (Skov, 2005). According to the International Fur Trade Federation (I.F.T.F.), by 2007, global fur sales had increased for an eighth consecutive year, reaching $15 billion (International Fur Trade Federation, 2008). However, the global financial slowdown that began in 2008 appears to have affected the industry. Evidence includes auctions at Kopenhagen Fur in Denmark, one of the world's largest fur auction houses, where pelt prices in 2009 were down about 30 percent from 2008 (Etter, 2009).

The **antifur movement** has been particularly strong in Britain, where it led to a total ban on fur farming in 2003 (Kerswell, 2009). Many top British designers refuse to include fur in their lines, including Vivienne Westwood, who went fur-free in 2006 ("Humane Society," 2006). Top designers in the United States, such as Calvin Klein, Ralph Lauren, and Tommy Hilfiger, have also pledged to go fur-free. Despite these designers' pledges and of the national ban, Kerswell (2009) claimed that the fur trade did not decline in Britain, and, according to some fur retailers, Britain is one of the fastest-growing markets for fur products in the world (Jagger, 2007).

People for the Ethical Treatment of Animals (PETA) and Friends of Animals are two animal advocacy groups that lobby against the use of fur in fashion. PETA, founded in 1980 and the largest animal rights group in the world, is a U.S. nonprofit organization. It is supported by two million members, including celebrities such as Paul McCartney, Pamela Anderson, and Sarah Jessica Parker. The organization is known for its aggressive media campaigns claiming, "Animals are not ours to eat, wear, experiment on, or use for entertainment." Several supermodels have posed naked alongside PETA's slogan "I'd rather go naked than wear fur" (Skov, 2005).

It has been argued that fur is a sustainable resource that is more environmentally friendly than oil-based synthetic fibers (Skov, 2005). In fact, some sector of the trade are now pushing fur as a green product to U.K. consumers, despite the chemicals used to treat fur, the feed for the animals, the necessary transportation to slaughter, the massive energy consumption in the industry, and other waste associated with the industry, including slurry, bedding, and animal corpses (Jagger, 2007). In addition, farmed fur requires twenty times the energy needed to produce faux fur ("Fake vs. vintage," 2008). Like fur, leather is also renewable and is fully biodegradable because it comes from organic sources; however, leather products require dry cleaning that uses chemicals such as perchloroethylene, trichlorofluoromathane, or trichlorotrifluoroethane, which are toxic to humans and harmful to the environment ("Dry cleaning," 2002). As alternatives, the popularity of **fake fur and leather** has been on the rise. The best fake fur tends to be made of fine acrylic fibers. Acrylic can be dyed to represent the colors and patterns of real animals (Ellis-Christensen, 2010). Fake fur can give a certain amount of warmth to a garment, although it is not as warm as real fur. In recent years, washable suede garments have also been commercially available (Chen & Burns, 2006).

There is also a growing market in vintage fur because some see this as a guilt-free way of wearing fur. While that is partly true, there is still a danger that glamorizing and increasing the visibility of fur will lead to greater demand (Kerswell, 2009). Given the increasing attention paid to animal welfare, the fur industry might not have a long future (Fur industry, n.d.).

Consumer trends toward recycled fashion

The textile recycling industry is one of the most established recycling industries in the world (Council for Textile Recycling, 1997) and consists of more than five hundred businesses (Hawley, 2006). The average American throws away roughly sixty-eight pounds of clothing and textiles per year, and about 85 percent of this waste goes to landfills (Dickson, Loker, & Eckman, 2009). In fact, analysis of municipal solid waste indicates that textile waste contributes to approximately 4.5 percent of U.S. landfills (Hammer, 1993). To combat this, the textile recycling industry diverts more than 1.25 million tons of postconsumer textile waste annually (Council for Textile Recycling, 1997). In addition, this industry diverts approximately 75 percent of the preconsumer textile waste from landfills into recycling centers (Chen & Burns, 2006).

The reuse, refurbishing, and recycling of fibers, fabrics, and garments can be a profitable as well as a sustainable business practice. For example, polyester has been extensively recycled to reduce its accumulation in landfills. Producing fibers from recycled polyester generates significantly less environmental pollution (by 85%) than does the production of polyester fibers made from new raw materials (Chen & Burns, 2006). In addition to the recycling potential of the fabric, polyester can be produced from recycled soda bottles made of polyethylene terephthalate (Chen & Burns, 2006). However, the quality of recycled polyester may not be as good as that of the virgin material (Kadolph, 2007).

Patagonia has been a leader in promoting recycling and environmentally sound material choices. In the early 1980s, a collaboration between Patagonia and Malden Mills led to a technological breakthrough in reuse and recycling: soda pop bottles were melted down to a basic polymer, extruded into fiber, and knitted into fleece (Loker, 2008). In 2005, Patagonia partnered with Japan's Teijin Group, which had, in 1999, developed ECO CIRCLE®, a closed-loop fiber-to-fiber recycling system that returns used fabric to its fiber state to be reused. Together, they initiated the Common Threads Recycling Program, through which customers voluntarily return worn-out Capolene® garments to Patagonia to be returned to the fiber state using the ECO CIRCLE® process. These fibers are then fashioned into new garments (Loker, 2008). According to Teijin's ECO CIRCLE®, the recycled polyester fiber is almost indistinguishable from new "virgin" polyester.

Burlington, one of the largest denim producers in the United States, has also undertaken several initiatives to make its production processes environmentally friendly. In 1993, it developed a program that allowed it to meet consumer demand but reduced the amount of denim waste going to municipal landfills. The company's Denim Division worked with researchers from North Carolina State University's College of Textiles to develop a new product, called Reused Denim™. To manufacture Reused Denim™, scrap denim is broken down into its component fibers and rewoven as denim yarn, which is used as the raw material for blue jeans. The new product consists of 50 percent virgin cotton yarn and 50 percent reused denim yarn (Sanguinetti, Lulofs, Lynn, & Newbold, 1997).

Sustainability has also become an emerging and growing issue in Brazil. Emilie Whitaker, designer of the denim brand Beija-Flor, has stated that Brazilian jeans companies are striving to achieve social and environmental goals by recycling denim scraps and reusing leftover fabrics. She also mentioned that her denim manufacturer is the largest water-recycling company in Brazil (Burford, 2009). The Brazilian jeans manufacturer Tristar recently introduced a new line of environmentally conscious jeans. Not only are the jeans made entirely of organic cotton, but the way they are cleaned is also eco-friendly. Instead of using a wasteful washing machine to clean these jeans, consumer can put them in a freezer for twenty-four hours to kill the bacteria, and the repeated thawing of the frozen jeans helps soften the fibers so that they become more form-fitting. In addition to the unorthodox method of cleaning, the jeans are completely reversible, which extends the time between cleanings. The company is also careful to be sustainable in its production processes. Its cotton is organically grown in Brazil on a plantation that uses no water or pesticides. Although efforts toward sustainability are its priority, the company believes that fashion and comfort will be its selling point (Messenger, 2010).

The market for recycled fashion created from postconsumer recycled textiles or garments is growing and has begun to receive increasing attention from consumers. Designers such as Miguel Adrover, GGrippo for trash-a-porter, Koi, and Ynnub have innovatively reconfigured Burberry coats, mattresses, t-shirts, jeans, and suits (Young, Jirousek, & Ashdown, 2004). Additionally, the designer Tierra Del Forte, for Del Forte Denim, has integrated a model, called Project Rejeaneration, for new consumerism within her business. Consumers send their used jeans back to the company after they have tired of them, and the company refreshes and produces a second generation of new products from them (Ulasewicz, 2008a).

Young, Jirousek, and Ashdown (2004) conducted a study in 1999 regarding the collection "Undesigned" (see Figure 6.3). The collection was designed for urban nomads, a demographic consisting of people who live in urban areas and who commute using ecologically sensitive public and human-powered modes of transportation. The researchers discussed sustainable design methods that incorporate the use of postconsumer recycled clothing and materials. The key concept for the project was described as "undesigned," which emphasized "the quality of the garments as deconstructed and reconstructed or undesigned and redesigned objects with a prior history, as opposed to conventionally designed and produced clothing" (p. 61). The authors argued that the project, as a response to the sustainable design movement

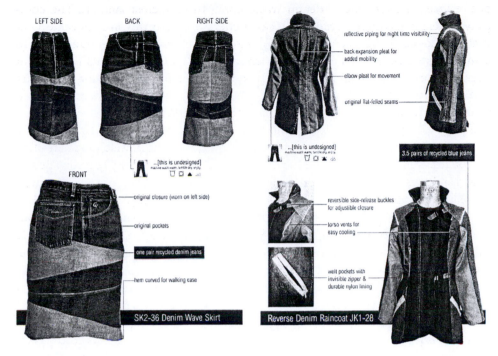

Figure 6.3 Young's recycled garment collection "Undesigned."

Source: Young, C. (2001). Undesigned: A study using postconsumer recycled clothing in the apparel design process. Unpublished master's thesis, Cornell University, Ithaca, NY.

that emerged in the 1990s, uncovered the need to completely rethink design, production, and the use of materials and resources in a way that is beneficial to both the environment and the people.

One preconception of recycled fashion is that it is not stylish or fashionable. However, an increasing appreciation for vintage styles is driving consumers not only to thrift stores but to high-street shops like Liberty and Marks and Spencer; moreover, new outlets such as high-end secondhand stores have appeared (Ulasewicz, 2008a). In recent years, a growing number of designers have created recycled high fashion presented in fashion shows. Linda Loudermilk, a California designer, launched her line Luxury Eco with the goal of creating a fabulous eco-fashion to convey the message that eco can be edgy, feminine, playful, and hyper-cool (Loudermilk, n.d.). Figure 6.4 shows an example of a feminine, chic wedding ensemble redesigned from a puffy wedding dress and reconstructed with handmade silk flowers for the SS 06 collection by Undesigned. In this section, various examples of recycled fashion were discussed. Case 6.2 provides an example Nike, a company that makes fabric from recycled soda bottles and polyester manufacturing waste. Also, Activity 6.1 and Activity 6.2 provide opportunities to explore sustainable fashion trends.

Figure 6.4 Wedding ensemble, redesigned from a puffy wedding dress and reconstructed with handmade silk flowers, for the SS 06 collection by Undesigned.
Source: Carol Young.

CASE 6.2. FABRICS MADE FROM RECYCLED SODA BOTTLES AND POLYESTER MANUFACTURING WASTE

Nike has made a long-term commitment to eliminate waste. In 2010 at the World Cup in South Africa, for the first time ever, all of Nike's national teams including Brazil, Portugal, The Netherlands, U.S.A., and South Korea were wearing jerseys made entirely from recycled polyester. Each garment was produced from up to eight recycled plastic bottles. Nike's fabric suppliers utilized discarded plastic bottles from Japanese and Taiwanese landfills, melting them down to produce new yarn that was ultimately converted to fabric for the jerseys. Charlie Denson, President of Nike Brand, said, "With today's announcement, we are equipping athletes with newly designed uniforms that not only look great and deliver performance benefits, but are also made with recycled materials, creating less impact on our environment." This process saves raw materials and reduces energy consumption by up to 30% compared to manufacturing virgin polyester. By using recycled polyester for its national jerseys, Nike prevented nearly 13 million plastic bottles, nearly 254,000 kg of polyester waste in total, from going into landfills. The national team jerseys represent an important step in the process of making all Nike products sustainable.

Source

Recycled shirts to star at soccer World Cup. (2011, July 15). *Ecotextile News*. Retrieved from http://www.ecotextile.com/news_details.php?id=10114

ACTIVITY 6.1. FINDING HIGH-TECH FIBERS MADE FROM RENEWABLE SOURCES

In recent years, numerous high-tech fibers have been developed and applied to apparel. The fibers have been increasingly used in wearable technology garments to provide enhanced function. An example is "smart fibers" that automatically heat and adjust to body temperature. What high-tech fibers are made from renewable sources? Find three examples of the fibers, and describe their applications to apparel.

ACTIVITY 6.2. DESIGNING A SUSTAINABLE GARMENT COLLECTION

There are numerous ways to create a sustainable garment collection. Consider all the aspects of creating a garment—materials, design, and production. For example, you can use sustainable materials, such as green or recycled fiber or fabrics or fake fur. You can consider dyeing fabric with natural materials, such as vegetables, or you can deconstruct a recycled garment and then redesign and construct a new garment. You can also consider a design that wastes minimal fabric. Create a collection of five garment designs for the next season. First, briefly describe a theme, and include a title for the collection. Second, describe the process ideas used to promote sustainability. Finally, sketch the designs

Minimum-fabric-waste fashion in design and product development processes

Although sustainability has become an increasingly crucial issue in the apparel industry, there has been relatively limited discussion of how to integrate it into apparel design and product development processes. Rather, many discussions have focused on sustainable materials and the manufacturing process, when, in fact, most factors that have environmental impacts are determined at the design stage. Thus, design has a central role to play in achieving a sustainable future (Chapman & Gant, 2007).

First, the amount of fabric waste is determined by garment and pattern design, depending on the shapes and number of pattern pieces. According to Rissanen (2008), 15 percent of total fabric on average ends up as waste. In the late 1990s, Issey Miyake and Dai Fujiwara launched A-POC (A Piece of Cloth), knitting a flat tube of fabric with the two sides of the tube joined in some areas (see Figure 6.5). A-POC is made using an industrial knitting or weaving machine programmed by a computer. This process creates continuous tubes of fabric. The consumer buys a tube and, following the lines of the joints, cuts out the finished garment exactly to the length he or she wants (Kries & Vegesack, 2001). This interactive new method not only reduces leftover fabric but also permits the consumer to participate in the final step of the design of their garment. With A-POC, mass production and custom-made clothing are integrated into one through the use of technology and imaginative thinking (Miyake & Fujiwara, 2010).

Similar to A-POC, a seamless knitting process uses one piece of yarn to complete an entire garment without cutting or sewing. The reduced yarn waste and the lack of waste from cutting eliminate excess fabric. This process also reduces the amount of garment flow in the fashion system by its mass-customization characteristics; it can be used to make one garment at a time, responding to a customer's design needs with quick-response production (Loker, 2008).

Figure 6.5 A-POC (A Piece of Cloth) by Issey Miyake.
Source: Scanlon, J. (2004). Seamless. *Wired, 12*(4). Retrieved from http://www.wired.com/wired/archive/12.04/miyake.html. Photographed by Stan Musilek.

The most common way to minimize fabric waste in garment and pattern design processes is to use rectangular pattern shapes. In this case, fit can be achieved with drawstrings or belts. Additionally, these garments can be sold at reduced prices because they require the minimal sewing (Rissanen, 2008). For example, Australian designer Mark Liu created a strapless dress for his zero-fabric-waste garments by designing the garment pattern and the printed textile simultaneously. Through cutting and sewing, the entire textile piece becomes the dress with no fabric waste. Another designer, Yeohlee Teng, in New York, strives for economical fabric use as her signature for her work (Rissanen, 2008).

The contribution of Internet information to socially responsible consumer decisions

The Internet has quickly grown to become a global business resource. By January 2000, 72 million host computers around the world were connected to the Internet, enabling 260 million people to go online (Brown, Renner, & Halweil, 2000). The number of Internet users in the world grew by 444.8 percent from 2000 to 2010; the number of users around the world reached nearly two billion by June 2010, with the highest number of users in Asia (825 million), followed by Europe (475 million), and the United States (266 million) (Internet World Stats, 2010). In 2001, in the United States, more than thirty million households were online surfing the net and purchasing products and services (Reisch, 2001); by May 2010, 79 percent of American adults used the Internet, according to Pew Internet's 2010 survey (Pew Internet, 2010). Reisch (2001) argued that the Internet's potential lies in facilitating the worldwide exchange of ideas, knowledge, and contacts and increasing consumer-citizen empowerment. The Internet's potential impact on and its possible role with regard to sustainable consumption patterns have been studied (Michaelis, 2000; Reisch, 2001). According to Michaelis (2000), the Internet affects consumers in a number of ways: it is a source of information on the social and environmental impact of consumption choices; it has an agenda-setting and gatekeeping function for public discourse and hence indirectly influences consumers' opinions, habits, and actions; it directly influences consumer behavior by educating people on how to be a good consumer; it functions as a feedback mechanism, reinforcing aspects of consumer culture; and it has structural effects on relationships, on real and virtual community building, and hence on consumption.

At the turn of the twentieth century, many companies believed that eco-intelligent products and services might become successful through Web-based (niche) eco-marketing (Reisch, 2001). Virtual shopping malls for eco-fair products and green e-portals as gatekeepers appeared, allowing for pre-selection, direct search, and purchase (Nachtmann & Kolibius, 2000). The Center for Remanufacturing and Reuse (C.R.R.) in the United Kingdom launched a new project in 2009 to improve current reuse levels of corporate clothing in a bid to divert waste from British landfills, where some 1.2 million tons of textiles are dumped each year. The main output of the project was an online resource with information and tools to educate consumers and increase their awareness of barriers and opportunities with regard to the reuse of corporate wear garments. The Web site includes a database of alternative fibers suitable for corporate wear, including options for reuse and recycling at end of life; case studies of best practices; and a searchable database of companies. The project is currently looking for examples of corporate wear take-back and reuse or recycling schemes from around the world. C.R.R. consultant Fiona Kelday says, "We are interested in companies which have improved the sustainability of the corporate wear garments that they buy, manufacture, supply and dispose of. . . . If anyone has a great story to tell in relation to these areas we would love them to get in touch" ("Defra-backed group," 2008). There are a growing number of international organizations like C.R.R. that support sustainability. One example is the international nonprofit organization Sustainable Style Foundation (S.S.F.), which was founded to provide information, resources, and innovative programs that promote sustainable living and sustainable design.

While the potential of the Internet to support sustainable lifestyles is promising, several counterproductive effects have been named (Reisch, 2001). First, there is the concern regarding a dramatic increase in demand for electricity and materials. Further, the manufacturing of personal computers causes enormous ecological harm, especially the manufacturing of semiconductors, which involves a number of questionable solvents and chemicals. Additionally, personal computers are relatively short-lived and are problematic to discard, and the personal computer industry is one of the most electricity-intensive industries in the world (Mills, 1999). Complete Activity 6.3, which will give you an opportunity to reflect on the contribution of Internet information to socially responsible consumption.

ACTIVITY 6.3. IDENTIFYING THE CONTRIBUTION OF INTERNET INFORMATION TO SOCIALLY RESPONSIBLE CONSUMPTION

Reflect on your purchases of apparel or accessory items over the past two years. Which products were socially responsible or examples of sustainable consumption? Provide two examples, along with the reasons why those purchases were socially responsible consumptions. Then, describe what information you found and used from the Internet and where you found it. How did the information affect your decision regarding the purchases? Did the information educate you on sustainable and socially responsible consumption? Briefly describe what you learned.

Cost issues associated with environmental improvements and programs to encourage socially responsible firms

With their growing sensitivity toward social and environmental issues, business executives recognize that long-term economic growth is not achievable unless that growth is socially and environmentally sustainable (Epstein, 2008). Epstein (2008) argued that a balance among economic progress, social responsibility, and environmental protection provides a competitive advantage to a firm. Recent research has shown a strong and positive connection between successful sustainability strategies and corporate value. Sustainability can enhance businesses in several ways (Bansal & Roth, 2000; Savitz & Weber, 2006). These include financial payoffs (e.g., increased revenue), customer-related payoffs (e.g., increased customer satisfaction, improved brand reputation, new market opportunities), operational payoffs (e.g., process innovation, productivity gains, reduced product cycle times), and organizational payoffs (e.g., increased employee satisfaction, improved stakeholder relationships, reduced regulatory intervention) (Epstein, 2008).

However, developing and implementing sustainability strategies is a challenge for many senior executives (Epstein, 2008). These managers are confronted with the paradox of simultaneously improving social, environmental, and financial performance, the three elements that make up sustainable performance. Epstein (2008) claimed that companies are investing large sums of money in sustainability programs, which require technological improvements. To make sound investment and strategy implementation decisions regarding sustainability, costs and benefits must be identified and measured. Unfortunately, most companies do not have an adequate system for identifying and measuring the social and environmental impact of new products, processes, and facilities. Some companies do not separately track or monitor social and environmental costs; thus, they do not know their total costs. Furthermore, the costs for sustainability are constantly changing. Even when sustainability is thought to provide financial benefits, the benefits can be measured only over long time spans, which make it difficult to determine the impact on social and environmental performance and to quantify the resulting benefits (Epstein, 2008).

Programs to recognize firms for exemplary sustainability performance

There are industry-wide award programs that currently provide recognition for companies that invest in sustainability. For example, in 1992, the American Textile Manufacturers Institute (A.T.M.I.) launched its Encouraging Environmental Excellence (E3) program to promote environmental awareness. To qualify for the E3 award, companies must meet ten requirements, such as having a corporate policy in support of the environment, having detailed environmental audits of their facilities, and developing employee education and community outreach programs (Dickerson, 2003). This program was eliminated when the A.T.M.I. was dismantled, in 2004. Since then, two leading national textile industry groups, the National Textile

Association (N.T.A.) and the National Council of Textile Organization (N.C.T.O.), have revived the E3 program (Orzada & Moore, 2008).

The Sustainable Style Foundation (S.S.F.) also supports the Outstanding Sustainable Style Achievement (O.S.S.A.) awards to recognize outstanding social and environmental efforts across the many style and design industries. These awards showcase the quantity and breadth of sustainability efforts under way in style industries and foster cross-industry awareness and inspiration. This is one of a few places where style makers, community organizations, businesses, and government come together to celebrate positive changes in the world (Sustainable Style Foundation, 2006).

DuPont was awarded the Carbon Green Chemistry Award from the U.S. Environmental Protection Agency for its Bio-PDO™ materials following the company's 2005 placement on *Business Week*'s list of "The Top Green Companies" (Epstein, 2008). DuPont's sustainability strategy is an excellent example of an environmentally smart business model, especially considering that DuPont had been labeled the top U.S. polluter in the mid-1990s (Laszlo, 2008).

Forward-thinking companies have developed programs that provide awards to employees for exemplary sustainability performance. For example, Seiko, a Japanese-based manufacturer of watches, has established a prize to recognize employees' environmental contributions. It offers an incentive to implement sustainability and to align the interests of the corporation, senior managers, and all employees (Epstein, 2008). Activity 6.4 allows you to identify examples of these programs.

ACTIVITY 6.4. FINDING PROGRAMS THAT ENCOURAGE SOCIALLY RESPONSIBLE BUSINESS

Search for two programs that recognize a firm's efforts to achieve socially responsible and sustainable business ethics. Describe each program. What organizations support the programs? What firms have been recipients? In addition, find two examples of apparel/textile firms' recognition of their employees for outstanding sustainable actions.

Chapter Summary

- Change is an essential component of fashion, and its process inevitably produces waste. Moreover, with the advent of fast-fashion retailers, our garments have increasingly become more disposable. In this era of fast, disposable fashion, both designers and consumers must consider the problem of postconsumer waste.

- The social trend toward sustainability and social responsibility is gaining momentum, and this has influenced fashion trends in various ways, including trends toward green products, against using real fur or leather, and toward recycled fashion. Interest in minimum-fabric-waste design and product development is also growing.
- The potential impact and role of the Internet in furthering socially responsible consumer decisions have become an important topic. The Internet communicates the social and environmental impact of consumption choices and provides education about how to be a good consumer. The Internet also sets an agenda and acts as a gatekeeper for public discourse, influencing consumer opinions and actions. In addition, it functions as a feedback mechanism and reinforces aspects of consumer culture.
- There are emerging programs that recognize firms for exemplary sustainability performance. The American Textile Manufacturers Institute (A.T.M.I.) launched its Encouraging Environmental Excellence (E3) program in 1992 to encourage reducing, reusing, and recycling; unfortunately, it was eliminated in 2004.

Key Terms

- Antifur movement
- Bamboo
- Biodegradable
- Environmental friendliness
- Fake fur/leather
- Fast fashion
- Green
- Hemp
- Landfills
- Mass customization

- Minimum-fabric-waste fashion
- Natural dyes
- Organic cotton
- Recycling
- Redesign
- Social responsibility
- Sustainability
- Sustainable design
- Waste

Questions for review and discussion

1. What factors are accelerating the increase of waste in the apparel and textile industry? Consider all supply chains of the industry, in materials, design, production, and retailing.
2. What factors are influencing a reduction of waste in the apparel and textile industry? In particular, what are the contributions of various technologies to reducing waste in the process of creating and consuming garments? Describe in detail the role of each technology identified in reducing waste.
3. What other influences do sustainability and social responsibility have on fashion trends (not including those discussed in this chapter: consumer trends toward green products and recycled fashion, against the use of real fur or leather, and toward minimum-fabric-waste fashion)?

Suggested Readings

Dickson, M. A., & Eckman, M. (2006). Social responsibility: The concept as defined by apparel and textile scholars, *Clothing & Textiles Research Journal, 24*(3), 178–191.

Dickson, M. A., Loker, S., & Eckman, M. (2009). *Social responsibility in the global apparel industry.* New York: Fairchild Publications.

Hethorn, J., & Ulasewicz, C. (2008). *Sustainable fashion: Why now?* New York: Fairchild Publications.

Young, C., Jirousek, C., & Ashdown, S. (2004). Undesigned: A study in sustainable design of apparel; using post-consumer recycled clothing. *Clothing & Textiles Research Journal, 22*(1/2), 61–78.

References

Bansal, P., & Roth, K. (2000). Why companies go green: A model of ecological responsiveness. *Academy of Management, 43*(4), 717–736.

Baugh, G. (2008). Fibers: Clean and green fiber options. In J. Hethorn & C. Ulasewicz (Eds.), *Sustainable fashion: Why now?* (pp. 326–357). New York: Fairchild Publications.

Blackburn, R. S. (2005). *Biodegradable and sustainable fibres.* Cambridge, England: Woodhead Publishing.

Brown, L. R., Renner, M., Halweil, B., & Stark, L. (2000). *Vital signs 2000–2001: The environmental trends that are shaping our future.* London: Earthscan.

Burford, L. (2009). Interview with Beija-Flor designer Emilie Whitaker. *DenimBlog.* Retrieved from http://www.denimblog.com/interviews/interview-with-beija-flor-designer-emilie-whitaker/

Carroll, A. (1999). Corporate social responsibility. *Business & Society, 38*(3), 268–295.

Chapman, J., & Gant, N. (2007). *Designers, visionaries and other stories.* London: Earthscan.

Chen, H-L., & Burns, L. D. (2006). Environmental analysis of textile products. *Clothing & Textiles Research Journal, 24*(3), 248–261.

China Bambro Textile Co. (2003). Bambro tex technical guidance. Retrieved from http://www.bamboo-t-shirt.com/bambrotextech.pdf

Council for Textile Recycling. (1997). Don't overlook textiles! Retrieved from http://www.textilerecycle.org/

Defra-backed group begins "Uniform Reuse" project. (2008, September 2). letsrecycle.com. Retrieved from http://www.letsrecycle.com/news/latest-news/textiles/defra-backed-group-begins-uniform-reuse-project

Dickerson, K. G. (2003). *Inside the fashion business* (7th ed.). Upper Saddle River, NJ: Pearson Education.

Dickson, M. A., & Eckman, M. (2006). Social responsibility: The concept as defined by apparel and textile scholars. *Clothing & Textiles Research Journal, 24*(3), 178–191.

Dickson, M. A., Loker, S., & Eckman, M. (2009). *Social responsibility in the global apparel industry.* New York: Fairchild Publications.

Dry cleaning of leather garments. (2002). Retrieved from http://www.fenice.com/dry_cleaning.html

Ellis-Christensen, T. (2010, April 16). What is faux fur? Wise geek. Retrieved from http://www.wisegeek.com/what-is-faux-fur.htm

Epstein, M. J. (2008). *Making sustainability work.* Sheffield, UK: Greenleaf Publishing.

Etter, L. (2009, February 12). Slowing economy pelts the global fur business. *The Wall Street Journal.* Retrieved from http://online.wsj.com/article/SB123439872449675207

Fletcher, K. (2008). Clothes that connect. In J. Chapman & N. Grant (Eds.), *Sustainable fashion and textiles: Design journeys.* London: Earthscan.

Frings, G. (2005). *Fashion: From concept to consumer*. Upper Saddle River, NJ: Pearson.

Fur industry. (n.d.). *BBC News Round*. Retrieved from http://news.bbc.co.uk/cbbcnews/hi/find_out/guides/animals/fur_industry/newsid_2459000/2459451.stm

Gap Inc. (2007, March 20). Organic cotton t-shirt debut at Gap. *The Corporate Responsibility Newswire*. Retrieved from http://www.csrwire.com/press_releases/25693-Organic-Cotton-T-Shirts-Debut-at-Gap

Hammer, M. (1993). *Home environment*. Gainesville: University of Florida Press.

H&M to launch sustainable collection. (2010, March 26). *Ecotextile News*. Retrieved from http://www.ecotextile.com/news_details.php?id=10134

Hawley, J. M. (2006). Digging for diamonds: A conceptual framework for understanding reclaimed textile products. *Clothing & Textiles Research Journal, 24*(3), 262–275.

Hethorn, J., & Ulasewicz, C. (Eds.). (2008). *Sustainable fashion: Why now?* New York: Fairchild Publications.

How to recycle everything wrong. (2009, December 1). Best green tips. Retrieved from http://www.bestgreenhometips.com/author/jennifer/

Human Society of the United States. (2006). Vivien Westwood latest fashion designer to go fur-free. Press release. Retrieved from http://hsus.org/press_and_publications/press_releases/vivien_westwood_latest.html

International Fur Trade Federation. (2008). Retrieved from http://www.iftf.com/ifftf_3_1_1.phpid=160

Internet World Stats. (2010). World Internet usages statistics: The Internet big picture. Retrieved from http://www.internetworldstats.com/stats.htm

Jagger, S. (2007, December 3). Price of mink nears record but ethical row over fur trade continues, *The Times*. Retrieved from http://business.timesonline.co.uk/tol/business/markets/united_states/article3111702.ece

Kadolph, S. J. (2007). *Textiles* (10th ed.). Upper Saddle River, NJ: Prentice Hall.

Kaiser, S. (2008). Mixing metaphors in the fiber, textile, and apparel complex: Moving toward a more sustainable fashion system. In J. Hethorn & C. Ulasewicz (Eds.), *Sustainable fashion: Why now?* (pp. 139–164). New York: Fairchild Publications.

Kelly, N. (2003). Will corn revolutionized the fiber industry? The costume gallery. Retrieved from http://www.costumegallery.com/Textiles/corn.html

Kerswell, J. (2009). Fashion crimes: The cruelty of the fur industry. Retrieved from http://www.scribd.com/doc/30123696/The-cruelty-of-the-fur-industry

Kim, H. S., & Damhorst, M. L. (1998). Environmental attitude and apparel consumption. *Clothing & Textiles Research Journal, 16*(3), 126–133.

Kries, M., & Vegesack, A. (2001). *A-Poc making. Issey Miyake & Dai Fujiwara*. Berlin: Vitra Design Museum.

Laszlo, C. (2008). *Sustainable value*. Sheffield, UK: Greenleaf Publishing.

Loker, S. (2008). A technology-enabled sustainable fashion system: Fashion's future. In J. Hethorn & C. Ulasewicz (Eds.), *Sustainable fashion: Why now?* (pp. 95–126). New York: Fairchild Publications.

Loudermilk, L. (2010). An example is a California designer Linda Loudermilk. Retrieved from http://www.lindaloudermilk.com

Menkes, S. (2006, May 31). Eco-friendly: Why green is the new black. *International Herald Tribune*.

Messenger, S. (2010, February 4). Green jeans: Forget washing. Just freeze them. *Fashion and Beauty*. Retrieved from http://www.treehugger.com/files/2010/02/green-jeans-forget-washing-just-freeze-them.php

Michaelis, L. (2000). The media: A resource for sustainable consumption. Workshop issues paper for a workshop at New College Oxford, January 8–9, 2001. Oxford: Commission on Sustainable Consumption.

Mills, M. P. (1999). The Internet begins with coal. A preliminary exploration of the impact of the Internet on electricity consumption. Arlington, VA: Greening Earth Society.

Miyake, I., & Fujiwara, D. (2001). A-POC Making. Retrieved from http://www.designboom.com/eng/funclub/apoc.html

Nachtmann, M., & Kolibius, M. (2000). Eco-e-commerce in business-to-consumer-bereich–das beispiel lebensmittelindustrie. In U. Schneidewind, A. Truscheit, & G. Steingräber (Eds.), *Nachhaltige Informationsgesellschaft* (pp. 83–109). Marburg: Metropolis.

Ortega, B. (1994, November 8). Organic cotton may feel soft to touch, but it's hard to sell. *The Wall Street Journal,* pp. B1, B18.

Orzada, B., & Moore, M. A. (2008). Environmental impact of textile production. In J. Hethorn & C. Ulasewicz (Eds.), *Sustainable fashion: Why now?* (pp. 299–325). New York: Fairchild Publications.

Pew Internet. (2010). Trend data. Retrieved from http://www.pewinternet.org/Trend-Data/Internet-Adoption.aspx

Pine, J. III. (1993). *Mass customization.* Boston: Harvard Business School Press.

Recycled shirts to star at soccer World Cup. (2011, July 15). *Ecotextile News.* Retrieved from http://www.ecotextile.com/news_details.php?id=10114

Reisch, L. A. (2001). The Internet and sustainable consumption: Perspectives on a Janus face. *Journal of Consumer Policy 24,* 251–286.

Rissanen, T. (2008). Creating fashion without the creation of fabric waste. In J. Hethorn & C. Ulasewicz (Eds.), *Sustainable fashion: Why now?* (pp. 184–206). New York: Fairchild Publications.

Rosenthal, E. (2007, January 25). Can polyester save the world? *The New York Times,* p. G-1.

Sanguinetti, G., Lulofs, F., Lynn, F., & Newbold, M. (1997). The Denim Division. In M. Newbold & G. Sanguinetti (Eds.), *Sustainable development in North Carolina* (pp. 4). Chapel Hill, NC: Burlington Industries, Inc.

Savitz, A. W., & Weber, K. (2006). *The triple bottom line.* San Francisco: Jossey-Bass.

Skov, L. (2005). The return of the fur coat: A commodity chain perspective. *Current Sociology 53*(1), 9–32.

Stern, N. Z., & Ander, W. N. (2008). *Greentailing and other revolutions in retail.* Hoboken, NJ: John Wiley & Sons, Inc.

Stevens, E. S. (2002). *Green plastics.* Princeton, NJ: Princeton University Press.

Sustainable Style Foundation. (2006, January 17). Look fabulous, live well, do good. Retrieved from http://www.sustainablestyle.org/about-ssf/

Sustainable Textile Standard. (n.d.). Retrieved from http://www.greenblue.org/activities_stm.html

Ulasewicz, C. (2008a). Fashion, social marketing, and the eco-savvy shopper. In J. Hethorn & C. Ullasewicz (Eds.), *Sustainable fashion: Why now?* (pp. 30–52). New York: Fairchild Publications.

Ulasewicz, C. (2008b). Martex Fiber Southern Corp, Eco2Cotton™ by Jimtex Yarns™, in2Green™. In J. Hethorn & C. Ulasewicz (Eds.), *Sustainable fashion: Why now?* (pp. 264–268). New York: Fairchild Publications.

Welters, L. (2008). The fashion of sustainability. In J. Hethorn & C. Ulasewicz (Eds.), *Sustainable fashion: Why now?* (pp. 7–29). New York: Fairchild Publications.

Young, C., Jirousek, C., & Ashdown, S. (2004). Undesigned: A study in sustainable design of apparel; using post-consumer recycled clothing. *Clothing & Textiles Research Journal, 22*(1/2), 61–78.

7

THE FORMAT OF TREND FORECASTS AND THE INFLUENCE OF TREND FORECASTING ON BUSINESS DECISIONS

Objectives

- Understand various formats of trend forecasts
- Understand the impact of leading-edge techniques on trend forecast formats
- Understand the influence of trend forecasting on business decisions

Formats for trend forecasts

Trend forecasting is a powerful tool that not only presents a reliable view of future trends but also gives apparel firms confidence that their creative business decisions are well informed. With the globalization of consumer markets, many apparel firms hire forecasting companies and also employ their own in-house forecasting teams. In general, trend services provide an overview of the season, including the following information: key changes in consumer attitudes; trends, including information about influencing factors behind the trends; and key design features, patterns, styling, materials, and color palette, which together provide a clear visual interpretation of the season's design themes. Forecasting companies disseminate information about trends through trend portfolios that include trend books, visual boards, slides, videos, and DVDs that provide projections of major trends in styles, fabrics, colors, patterns, accessories, and theme ideas (Swanson & Everett, 2000).

Brannon (2005) argued that, while identifying trends is necessary, it is only the first step in developing a trend forecast presentation. She emphasized that the process of sorting, organizing, and editing material and searching for relationships and patterns creates meanings that must be conveyed in any presentation. This section introduces different formats used for trend forecasts, such as trend maps, trend boards and other visual materials, oral presentations, and other leading-edge techniques.

Above all, a forecaster's task is to map uncertainty in a world where present actions influence the future. When looking at forecasts, it is easy to assume that they are predictions of what the future should be; however, they are more like a map of possible outcomes that you can use to reach a desired destination. The forecaster's job is to define the uncertainty in a manner that helps decision makers exercise strategic judgment. Many factors go into delineating the uncertainty, such as the relationships among its elements and the ranking of possible outcomes, but determining the breadth is the crucial first step (Saffo, 2007).

A **trend map** in the apparel industry identifies emerging, steadily growing, or declining trends. A trend map also draws distinctions between major trends that will appeal to large consumer groups and minor trends that will appeal to niche markets or small groups of consumer (Brannon, 2005). Determining the level of acceptance of each trend is also important. On the map, trends are classified as **trial balloons** (items, styles, or looks with which designers experiment to gauge the effect and potential of a new idea), **embryonic trends** (items, styles, or looks in the very first stages of development), and **directional trends** (styles or items adopted by fashion innovators or fashion-forward retailers) (Perna, 1987). Activity 7.1 provides an opportunity to practice identifying the three types of trends.

ACTIVITY 7.1. IDENTIFYING A TRIAL BALLOON, EMBRYONIC TREND, AND DIRECTIONAL TREND

Look at a minimum of twenty photos of apparel styles presented in fashion shows for the next season, and read at least five recent articles published in fashion magazines or posted on relevant Web sites related to upcoming trends. Identify one trial balloon, one embryonic trend, and one directional trend for the next season. Summarize and analyze your findings.

Trend board and other visual materials

Fashion forecasting companies report trend forecasts using specific formats. The forecasts include descriptions of themes, sketches of garment styles, fabric swatches, and color samples that they believe will be popular. They also publish consumer trends for particular target markets (Frings, 2008). Some companies offer one all-purpose edition of a trend report that discusses important developments in each segment of the fashion industry. Others take a more specialized approach and prepare individual **trend books** that concentrate on specific segments of fashion (e.g., men's sportswear, women's intimate wear) (Diamond & Diamond, 2008). Promostyl publishes individual trend books that report on color direction, textiles, prints, silhouettes, and styles, focusing on specific segments of fashion eighteen to twenty-four months in advance of each season. The reports include a series of drawings created by company artists and photographs from which the design inspirations were taken. Color chips and fabric swatches accompany and enhance each presentation for apparel and accessories classifications such as women's, men's, and children's wear. They clearly outline the direction in which the forecasters think that industry segment is headed (Stone, 2008). In addition to the trend books, the company publishes online products for its clients. Web sites are updated continually, whereas print publications may be obsolete soon after they are published and are not brought up to date until the next printing. Figure 7.1 shows multiple pages of trend books with various sources of inspiration, including theme keywords, color palettes, and fabrics created by PFIN, a fashion forecasting company in South Korea.

Trend boards are an essential component of trend reports. These are visual layouts that give a comprehensive overview of market behavior. They present trend directions, including styles, color, textile, print, and pattern inspirations (see Figure 7.2). Increasingly, digital trend boards are becoming more prominent (Trenzza Design Studio, n.d.). Digital trend boards work with PowerPoint presentations and can be used in virtual online meetings and presentations. Barbara Russillo, president of DML Marketing, which also makes Legale Legwear, said, "Trend boards are

Figure 7.1 Trend books with inspirations, including theme keywords, color palettes, and fabrics by PFIN.
Source: PFIN.

THE FORMAT OF TREND FORECASTS

Figure 7.2 A trend board with various sources of inspirations by PFIN.
Source: PFIN.

absolutely more important than they used to be. . . . Not everyone is very visual. The boards give vision to someone who might not have a lot of imagination. The visuals help the buyers buy appropriately for each delivery. . . . It helps them understand how their category relates to the realm of fashion. . . . It gives them more confidence about why they buy what they did" (Feitelberg, 1998).

Color boards offer a visual overview of new trends in color (see Figure 7.3). Predicted popular colors are developed into several different color palettes, including new directional colors, fashion-driven colors, and stable colors. These are presented with the inspiration sources, taking into consideration market directions, direct competitors, and customer preferences (Trenzza Design Studio, n.d.). Like trend boards, digital color boards can be used for PowerPoint presentations and virtual online presentations. **Mood** or **inspiration boards** are usually assembled on corkboards or in scrapbooks. These collages of magazine tear sheets, historic photos, fabric swatches, and snapshots serve as conceptual tools to present colors, textures, and themes of designers' new collections (see Figure 7.4). Mood board images tend to be more metaphorical than literal (Ferla, 2004). In other words, a mood board conveys an overall theme but does not necessarily predict the created garment design features. For example, if the theme of new garment collections is sustainability, a mood board can contain numerous images of nature.

Workbooks are in-depth publications that cover haute couture designs that lower-end designers and manufacturers use as styles guides. **Print and online newsletters** are other economical promotional sources to update clients on news of fibers and fabrics, styles and silhouettes, new colors, and hot items. Prominent forecasters

The color palette labels read:
SOURBALL
ESPRESSO
TRUFFLE
HIDE
EGGSHELL
ASPHALT
HALO
BLACK FOREST
ROUGE

©Poppy Gall Design 2009

Figure 7.3 A color board with a color palette and various sources of inspirations by Poppy Gall.
Source: Poppy Gall Design Studio. Retrieved from http://poppygall.com/blog/tag/color-trend/.

Figure 7.4 Mood boards by PFIN.
Source: PFIN.

also offer libraries of the fabrics and fibers available throughout the apparel industry. Although designers and manufacturers travel annually to trade shows around the world, subscribing to these services enables them to review the materials as needed (Stone, 2008).

In creating a trend board or any of the other type of boards we have discussed, you will need to consider the overall visual effect. A trend board should look organized and should be aesthetically pleasing. To achieve this goal, the principles of design (unity, balance, proportion, emphasis, rhythm) should be well applied as you employ the design elements of line, shape (form), texture (pattern), and color. The font types and text size, as well as the shapes and sizes of all other components, such as photos, color samples, and fabric swatches, should be carefully chosen. Layout is also crucial to the final results of a board and should be thoroughly planned before you put all the components of the board together. The layout of a trend board directs the way the viewer's eye takes in the content. A random arrangement can be confusing and unintelligible. An organized layout with an emphasis creates visual interest. Activity 7.2 provides an opportunity to create a trend board for a future fashion trend considering the guidelines mentioned above.

ACTIVITY 7.2. CREATING A TREND BOARD

This is a group activity, with each group consisting of three students. Read ten to fifteen articles on fashion trend or style forecasts published in recent fashion or trade magazines, and identify trend themes for the next season. Choose one theme, label it, and then create a trend board that identifies its mood or spirit, with a color palette, fabric swatches, and garment styles.

Oral presentation

In addition to offering individual consultations, forecasting companies provide seminars to professionals in the textile and apparel industry, so good **oral presentations** are essential. Studies (Patterson, 1983) find that public speaking is among people's greatest social fears, so the following tips may help if you are called on to make an oral presentation:

1. Know your audience. Tailor your presentation to your audience's knowledge of the subject and what it needs to know (Patterson, 1983). Many audiences are a mixed bag: some members are already experts on your topic, some are experts in the general area, and others know little or nothing about the topic. You need to think who needs to know what and provide material for everyone. Perhaps you can pitch the body of your talk to the experts, but make the introduction and the summary accessible to the entire audience (Hill, 1997).
2. Actively involve your audience. People's attention can wander easily if they do not connect to the topic. Work in some simple and quick questions you know audience members can answer. Provide analogies and anecdotes for examples, and, if you have a knack for it, use humor.

3. Use various **visual and audio aids** such as handouts, slides, video clips, and trend boards to supplement your information. Make sure everyone can easily see the visual aids (see Figure 7.4). **PowerPoint** is the world's most popular tool for public speeches. There are four hundred million copies of the software in circulation, and a typical PowerPoint slide contains forty words, about eight seconds' worth of silent reading. But PowerPoint is often misused or overused, so it is crucial to remember that visual aids should supplement what you have to say, not replace it. Don't use visual aids that are so complex that the audience will spend its time trying to read them instead of listening to you (Patterson, 1983).

4. Be clear. Remember, speaking is different from writing. Listeners have one chance to hear your talk and cannot rewind your live presentation when they get confused, and they usually have to wait until the end of the speech to ask questions. To communicate effectively, tell your audience what you are going to speak about at the beginning of the presentation and summarize what you told them at the end (Hill, 1997).

5. Be positive. Show that you are knowledgeable and enthusiastic about your subject. Speak with confidence. Maintain eye contact, and make certain you connect with everyone in the room so that they feel you are talking to them directly. Use natural hand gestures, but not to the point of distraction (Patterson, 1983).

Leading-edge techniques

As with every other aspect of our lives, advances in technology have affected the forecasting business. Global **digital communication** has radically expanded the variety of formats for trend forecasts. For example, DVDs are used to provide access to the runway shows and the latest street fashions from Paris, New York, or anywhere else in the world. Video is another ideal medium for fashion reporting. Videofashion News, which offers collection coverage and behind-the-scenes designer interviews, appears regularly on Style Network, USA Cable Network's Trio Popular Art Channel, and Cablevision's Metro TV. Videofashion News is even available on DVD (Frings, 2008). To communicate the latest seasonal trends, some forecasters develop video packages that cover silhouettes, styles, colors, fabrics, and patterns.

Countless fashion trend sources are scattered throughout cyberspace. Almost every major forecasting company, manufacturer, and retailer has a Web site (Frings, 2008). For retailers interested in private labeling, for example, the entire merchandising team can access sites to keep up on industry trends. In 2007, Promostyl embarked on a venture to provide information to its clients. A variety of products can be accessed online, making it easy for clients around the world to get up-to-the-minute information on trends and hot items as fast as the click of the mouse.

The growth of social networking sites allows nonindustry experts to post opinions and gain a following. Forecasters use these sites as a key source for mining information regarding consumer preferences. Companies from Best Buy to Louis Vuitton now consider social media a fundamental part of their marketing strategy. At the Cannes Lions International Advertising Festival 2010, Worth Global Style Network (WGSN) reported that social networking is vital to success in the industry (Arthur, 2010b). **Weblogs**, commonly known as blogs, are another increasingly necessary tool. Technorati, a blog search engine, tracked 35.5 million weblogs in 2007, with the number doubling every six months (Rickman & Cosenza, 2007). In 2006, two million blogs mentioned fashion specifically. Seventy-seven percent of blog readers are women, more than 49 percent are between the ages of twenty-two and thirty, more than 60 percent have a college degree, and 22 percent are students; these are demographics that exhibit tremendous interest in fashion and have significant spending power (Rickman & Cosenza, 2007). Three-quarters of global consumers use social networks and blogs, up 24 percent between April 2009 and April 2010, and 22 percent of online time is spent on social network or blog sites—one hit every four and a half minutes (Arthur, 2010b).

As **mobile devices** become increasingly indispensible consumer tools, with the number of shopping applications (or apps) (e.g., Frugalytics, Pongr Beta, Shopago) increasing exponentially, fashion marketers have taken notice. **Smart phones** are expected to overtake PC sales worldwide by 2012, and the future of marketing is increasingly going mobile. Mobile devices are far less expensive and, in many ways, far more convenient than desktop or laptop computers, and people from all demographics are now planning and organizing their lives via the handheld mobile device of their choice, whether for forging and maintaining relationships, keeping up with business and work, or redefining constant streams of entertainment, all of which ultimately relate directly to consumption. Therefore, it is important to understand the targeted audience well and learn how best to reach it. Speaking at Federated Media's CM Summit, Mary Meeker, of Morgan Stanley, a global financial services firm, said that marketing today comes down to finding "new ways to do old things faster, better, cheaper, and increasingly in the palm of your hand" (Arthur, 2010a).

The **iPad** is another innovation that has fueled the mobile wireless revolution. The iPad has innovative new software applications designed especially for it and is able to run most of the 140,000-plus existing **iPhone** apps. For example, "SketchyPad" is an app that allows you to sketch Web sites and make an interface of apps, including iPhone and iPad apps. This app will make designers', programmers', and interface designers' lives much easier. Easy-to-use interface and a variety of stencils will help users to mock up any Web sites and soft interfaces. Another app, "Digital Post," is a virtual newspaper for the iPad (Chapman, 2010). It allows users to receive hundreds of articles from dozens of sources through just one app without downloading a bunch of different newspaper apps. In 2010, ABC News announced the release of a new application for the Apple iPad, available in the Apple App Store. The new application takes full advantage of the form and functionality of the iPad, using as the principal navigation tool a unique interactive three-dimensional globe on which news stories appear. The launch of the ABC News iPad app marks the second time in recent months that the Disney/ABC Television Group has created an innovative video offering for the new platform. In April 2010, DATG became the first to bring ad-supported video to the iPad via the acclaimed ABC Player app, which has proven to be tremendously successful, with more than 928,000 downloads and 5.9 million episodes started in just over three months ("ABC news," 2010):

> iPad has provided a great impact on the fashion industry. Jefferson Hack told WGSN: The tablet revolution is a definite game-changer for fashion because fashion is about detail. When you start to be able to see detail, when you can get into really seeing high-quality moving images or still images, the fashion language can come alive. . . . The clothes, the texture, the fabric, the way they're worn, the way they move can really be seen, so someone can get an idea of what it is rather than have to make a guess. For me, it's the dawn of a new digital beauty. (Arthur, 2010c)

Gap, in collaboration with the digital agency AKQA, has been one of the first fashion retailers to launch its own app specifically for the iPad: "1969 stream." EDTI, an online trend service, uses the iPad as a trend platform (see Figure 7.5). Representatives from EDTI have noted some of the uses of these apps:

> iPad is perfect for fashion as a trend book with thousands of pages that you can zoom, organize and search, and will never be out of date. . . . You can actually touch our world-beating forecasts and Trend Science with your fingers. Pinch to

Figure 7.5 The iPad as a platform for trend forecasts used by EDITD, an online trend service.
Source: EDITD (2010). EDITD + iPad. Retrieved from http://editd.com/ipad/.

THE FORMAT OF TREND FORECASTS

zoom, touch to get colors, and browse around easily and quickly. It's the best platform for trend information we've used, ever. . . . You can hold a life-size picture of a pocket up against a garment and see how it looks. Or see a swatch in full size. Or place a print on a piece of fabric. (Arthur, 2010c)

The influence of trend forecasting on business decisions

Forecasting has a great influence on a number of important business decisions. In some cases, forecasts simply provide information, but, in many cases, they are the basis for major decisions, including what product lines to create, how much and in what ways to spend money on production, how aggressively to advertise or promote the products, and how best to get products to market in order to fulfill projected demand. A **sales forecast**, a prediction of a business's unit and dollars sales for some future period of time, may cause management to adjust some of its decisions about production and marketing if the forecast indicates that the current production capacity is grossly inadequate or excessive and if sales and marketing efforts are inconsistent with the expected outcomes. Forecasts give management the opportunity to examine a series of alternate plans for changes in resource commitments (such as plant capacity, promotional programs, and market activities), changes in prices, or changes in production scheduling ("Sales forecasting," n.d.). In this section, our discussion of the influence of trend forecasting on business decisions will focus on product **line development**, **promotion**, and ways to **minimize stock-out**.

Line development

Each season, designers work with merchandisers to develop new fashion lines. In very large apparel firms, such as Liz Claiborne and Levi Strauss, merchandisers are responsible for developing new lines. They review information on trends, colors, styles, fabrics, and other materials, often using fashion forecasting services (Stone, 2008). Merchandisers plan the overall fashion direction for the coming season and give directions to their design teams about seasonal themes, apparel items and accessories to be designed, and colors and fabrics to be used. In smaller companies, the owners or designers perform these tasks (Dickerson, 2003).

Each season, merchandisers must determine the number of groups and styles required to meet the demands of retailers and consumers and the financial goals of manufacturers. As discussed in chapter 4, the previous year's actual **sales records** are used as a basis for projecting sales goals for each group for the following year. Sales records are defined as the information a firm has on its customers, including their contact information, how often they purchase from the firm, what they purchase, and how they pay their bills ("Sales Records," 2010). Rising sales statistics show which products are increasingly widely adopted, while declines in sales suggest that styles have passed their peak in the fashion adoption curve. Weak sales may indicate that a style is not meeting consumer needs for any number of reasons related to fashion or quality. By carefully monitoring sales records, retailers project trends about everything from skirt and jacket lengths to whether customers prefer soft or tailored garments to what fabrics and colors will be in style (Frings, 2008).

The survival and growth of a retail chain depends on its ability to accurately forecast the sales volume for each item sold in each store to determine its future pricing, allocation and inventory. Despite such close monitoring, most U.S. retailers experience large errors in their sales forecasts, resulting in dramatic financial losses. According to the U.S. Census Bureau and National Retail Federation, U.S. retailers are losing more than $200 billion a year due to forecast errors (Kumar & Patel, 2008). Kumar and Patel (2008) proposed a clustering method in which various items are grouped on the basis of the similarity in their sales forecasts, after which a common forecast is computed for each cluster. On a real data set from a national retail chain, it was found that the proposed method of combining forecasts produced significantly better sales forecasts than either the individual forecasts (forecasts without combining) or an alternate method of using a single combined forecast for all items in a product line sold by the retailer.

To remain competitive and profitable, apparel product developers must respond to **consumer preferences**. They must be able to forecast subtle shifts in consumer preferences and create merchandise concepts that keep up with customers' wants and needs. On the basis of interviews with product developers, Brannon et al. (1993) found that access to relevant information from the apparel businesses was limited, and research efforts were casual among product developers. Brannon et al. investigated ways to improve the performance of product developers by enhancing access to relevant information, providing computer programs customized to specific tasks, and assessing the current state of forecasting theory and practice.

Two sources of information—point-of-sale (POS) data and consumer preference testing—are often cited as the best guides available to product developers. However, POS data show only what has sold at what price; they do not explain consumers' purchasing motivation, product satisfaction, or likely replacement behavior; neither do they report what consumers looked for but did not find. **Computer-integrated forecasting** using prototype hardware and software that captures, stores, organizes, and retrieves visual, verbal, and numerical data can provide competitive advantages: first, by providing continuous monitoring of information relevant to product development, including social and economic trends, fashion forecasts, apparel industry news, changes in strategy among competitors and partners, and shifts in consumer preferences; second, by enhancing decision making using knowledge-based systems and artificial intelligence; third, by helping managers understand forecasting theory, evaluating forecast providers, and customizing forecasting procedures for apparel manufacturers and merchandisers. Improving the success rate of new product introductions or line extensions by only a few percentage points can significantly increase profitability (Brannon et al., 1993).

In planning marketing strategies, the marketing director, fashion director, advertising director, visual merchandising director, merchandise manager, and buyer must agree on how to reach their target. At planning meetings, they discuss how to communicate fashion trends within the context of the store's image (Frings, 2008). The initial forecasts guide the development of the firm's marketing strategy (Ress & Snyder, 1994). From these forecasts, the store decides on specific price ranges, styles, and colors, chooses producers from which to purchase specific styles, and sets advertising campaigns for the season (Sproles & Burns, 1994). The fashion director or forecaster provides appropriate fashion information on upcoming trends, from buzz words to popular music, and images to use in creating ads that will highlight the season's theme. All of this is then turned over to the promotion department (Perna, 1987).

To test the projected forecasts, retailers bring merchandise into their stores two or three months ahead of the anticipated season. They begin advertising with an appropriate theme through signage, fashion shows, and other special events, pitching the new lines that consumers will soon see on the shelves and racks (Swanson & Everett, 2000). Often, such a storewide fashion theme involves a broad focus that can be used throughout the entire store, including the apparel and home furnishing departments. For example, a "sophisticated safari" theme may be featured in apparel departments for men, women, and children by incorporating khaki safari jackets with trousers, skirts, or shorts. The accessory department may add safari hats, knapsacks, tote bags, and sunglasses. The home store could contribute wicker picnic baskets, travel coolers, and linens. Virtually every department may contribute some products to the overall theme (Perna, 1987).

There is a strong mutual dependence between forecasting and promotion activities. Themes based on forecasts are important elements of promotional campaigns created far in advance of the actual selling season. These programs are the communication tool sellers use to announce upcoming trends early and often to the buying public (Swanson & Everett, 2000). Along with presenting upcoming trends to consumers through promotional channels, fashion forecasting depends on promotions as a major resource for predicting future trends.

Minimizing stock-out

Developing sound inventory strategies and managing them efficiently greatly affect profitability. Inventory is most likely the largest asset on a company's balance sheet. F. Curtis Barry & Company, known for operations consultancy, worked with a multichannel business to better understand its current fill rates and backorder issues. Fill rate is the percentage of customer orders satisfied from stock at hand, which is a measure of an inventory's ability to meet demand ("Fill Rate," n.d.). Backorders are customer orders that cannot be filled now and for which the customer is prepared to wait for some time while new inventory is acquired. The percentage of items backordered is an important measure of the effectiveness of a firm's inventory management ("Backorder," n.d.). F. Curtis Barry found that the company's cost to process backorders was more than $10 per unit, and the processing costs for all backorders were in excess of $750,000 annually. It recommended major changes to improve the accuracy of the initial planning, the reduction of backorders, increased turnover, and the use of analytical tools to evaluate items and promotions. These changes to the planning and purchasing processes led to a drop in the number of backorders and a reduction in processing costs by more than $200,000 without the addition of any additional staff (F. Curtis Barry & Company, 2010).

Demand forecasting requires an understanding of consumer demand for goods or services, which is predictive. Knowledge of how demand will fluctuate (e.g., on the basis of consumer adoption curves) enables suppliers to keep the right amount of stock on hand. If the company underestimates demand, sales will fall due to lack of supply. If it overestimates demand, suppliers will be left with surplus that can be a financial drain. The ability to accurately predict demand is imperative for companies that want to remain competitive in the marketplace, so it is important that they find a balance between the cost of running out of an item ($7–$12 per unit on backorders, according to proprietary studies) and the cost of overstock (margin loss from liquidating categories of product). To profitably meet consumer needs, appropriate forecasting models are vital. Although no model is flawless, unnecessary costs stemming from excessive or inadequate supply can often be avoided by the use of data-mining methods (StatSoft, n.d.). Case 7.1 illustrates how retailers analyze trends and make merchandising decisions to translate forecasts into sales in the fashion industry.

CASE 7.1. INTERVIEW WITH CAROLINE HIPPLE: TREND ANALYSIS TO MERCHANDISING DECISIONS

In her 30 years of experience in analyzing trends and making merchandising decisions for major multi-store retailers, Caroline Hipple enjoyed great success translating forecasts into sales. Now, as the leader of the brand management and consulting firm, hb2, she applies her expertise to assist retailers to create brands that coordinate marketing, merchandising, and sales models designed with the consumer in mind. "I recommend a systematized process of research in determining how to fit coming trends into your store" Hipple said. "To start, you can take advantage of online resources such as Michelle Lamb's The Trend Curve (www.trendcurve.com) and Robyn Waters' newsletter (www.rwtrend.com). Read trade publications, look at what's happening in the world of fashion and pay attention to the decorating ideas that are showing up on TV and in movies. At the High Point Market, the color and trend seminars and places like the Sherwin Williams showroom also provide excellent background information. As you gather your information, jot down the ideas that intrigue you, save tear-outs from the magazines and hang onto articles that you think are important. Then, you'll want to organize all of these inputs into an internal trend forecast, one that reflects your own point of view."

"Your forecast should contain four color/theme directions that will guide your merchandising over the coming season. Once you've decided on your directions, use color chips, textile samples, your magazine tear-outs and other images you've uncovered to create one board that visualizes each theme. You'll want to include a balance of elements on each board—subdued and neutral colors; dark and light tones; rough and smooth textures—so that each direction appeals to all of the senses. Your own, personal connection to the colors, styles or design elements you choose is critical. When you're deciding what new looks and products to add to your store, give your customers the new ideas and fresh inspirations they're seeking, but do it through subtle shifts, so that you maintain a consistent brand position regarding style."

Source

Fishman, M. (2005). Success in the city. *Atlanta in Town*. Retrieved from http://www.atlantaintownpaper.com/features/SuccessInCityHipple.php

Chapter Summary

- Trend maps identify emerging, steadily growing, or declining trends. Trend maps also draw distinctions between major trends that will appeal to large consumer groups and minor trends that will appeal to niche markets or small groups of consumers. Determining the level of acceptance of each trend is also important. On each map, trends are differentiated as trial balloons (items, styles, or looks with which designers experiment to gauge the effect and potential of a new idea), embryonic trends (items, styles, or looks in the very first stages of development), and directional trends (styles or items adopted by fashion innovators or fashion-forward retailers).

- Trend boards are visual layouts that give a comprehensive overview of market behavior. They present trend direction including silhouette, style, color, textile, and pattern. Increasingly, digital trend boards are becoming more prominent. Digital trend boards work with PowerPoint presentations and can be used in virtual online meetings and presentations.

- Forecasters use social networking sites as a key source for information-mining of consumer preferences. Weblogs are another increasingly necessary tool. As mobile devices become increasingly indispensible consumer tools, with shopping apps of all kinds increasing exponentially, fashion marketers have taken notice. The iPad is perfect for fashion as a trend book with thousands of pages that can be zoomed, organized and searched.

- Trend forecasting influences important business decisions such as line development, promotion, and minimizing stock-out. Each new season merchandisers review information on trends and plan the overall fashion direction for the coming season; then, they give directions to their design teams about seasonal themes, apparel items and accessories to be designed, and colors and fabrics to be used. Themes based on forecasts are also important elements of promotional campaigns created far in advance of the actual selling season. Also, accurate sales forecasting is a key to the survival and growth of an apparel business by minimizing stock-out and over-stock.

Key Terms

- Color board
- Computer-integrated forecasting
- Consumer preferences
- Digital communication
- Directional trend
- Embryonic trend
- iPad
- iPhone
- Line development
- Minimizing stock-out
- Mobile devices
- Mood board
- Newsletters (print and online)

- Oral presentation
- PowerPoint
- Promotion
- Sales forecast
- Sales records
- Smart phone
- Trend board
- Trend book
- Trend map
- Trial balloon
- Visual and audio aides
- Weblog
- Workbook

Questions for review and discussion

1. Discuss what makes a successful or poor trend board. Provide successful examples and poor examples of actual trend boards created by different apparel firms and analyze in detail the positive and negative elements.

Suggested Readings

Arthur, R. (2010c, May 14). The iPad: Gimmick or game-changer? WGSN Web site. Business Resource Features. Retrieved from http://www.wgsn.com/members/business-resource/research/br2010may14_091637

Brannon, E. L., Anderson, L. J., Ulrich, P. V., Trentham, G., Duffield, D., Padgett, M. L., & Marshall, T. (1993). Computer-integrated forecasting for demand-activated product development, manufacturing, and merchandising. *National Textile Center Annual Report.*

References

ABC news release innovative application for iPad. (2010, July 21). *ABC News.* Retrieved from http://blogs.abcnews.com/pressroom/2010/07/abc-news-releases-innovative-application-for-ipad.html

Arthur, R. (2010a, June 24). Mobil marketing: Internet Week New York insights. WGSN Web site. Business Resource Features. Retrieved from http://www.wgsn.com/members/business-resource/research/br2010jun24_092106

Arthur, R. (2010b, August 10). Social media in 2010: Steering the dialogue. WGSN Web site. Business Resource Features. Retrieved from http://www.wgsn.com/members/business-resource/research/br2010jul08_092301

Arthur, R. (2010c, May 14). The iPad: Gimmick or game-changer? WGSN Web site. Business Resource Features. Retrieved from http://www.wgsn.com/members/business-resource/research/br2010may14_091637

Brannon, E. L. (2005). *Fashion forecasting* (2nd ed.). New York: Fairchild Publications.

Brannon, E. L., Anderson, L. J., Ulrich, P. V., Trentham, G., Duffield, D., Padgett, M. L., & Marshall, T. (1993). Computer-integrated forecasting for demand-activated product development, manufacturing, and merchandising. *National Textile Center Annual Report.*

Backorder. (n.d.). *Business Dictionary.com.* Retrieved from http://www.businessdictionary.com/definition/backorder.html

Chapman, C. (2010, July 13). A blog completely dedicated to visual inspiration and sweet product round-ups. *The Inspiration Blog.* Retrieved from http://www.theinspirationblog.net/showcases/32-innovative-ipad-application-website- designs/

Diamond, J., & Diamond, E. (2008). *The world of fashion* (4th ed.). New York: Fairchild Publications.

Dickerson, K. G. (2003). *Inside the fashion business.* Upper Saddle, NJ: Pearson Education, Inc.

F. Curtis Barry & Company (2010). Forecasting and inventory management. Retrieved from http://fcbco.com/services/forecasting-inventory2.asp

Feitelberg, R. (1998, August 17). Trends boards make everything click. *Women's Wear Daily,* p. 10.

Ferla, R. (2004, February 8). Bless this mess. *The New York Times,* p. 1.

Fill Rate. (n.d.). *Business Dictionary.com.* Retrieved from http://www.businessdictionary.com/definition/fill-rate.html

Fishman, M. (2005). Success in the city. *Atlanta in Town.* Retrieved from http://www.atlantaintownpaper.com/features/SuccessInCityHipple.php

Frings, G. S. (2008). *Fashion from concept to consumer* (9th ed.). Upper Saddle, NJ: Pearson/Prentice Hall.

Hill, M. D. (1997, January). Oral presentation advice. Retrieved from http://pages.cs.wisc.edu/~markhill/conference-talk.html

Kumar, M., & Patel, N. R. (2010). Using clustering to improve sales forecasts in retail merchandising. *Annals of Operations Research, 174,* 33–46.

Mentzer, J. T., & Cox, J. E. (1984). Familiarity, application, and performance of sales forecasting techniques. *Journal of Forecasting, 3,* 27–36.

Patterson, D. (1983). How to give a bad talk. Retrieved from http://pages.cs.wisc.edu/~markhill/conference-talk.html#badtalk

Perna, R. (1987). *Fashion forecasting.* New York: Fairchild Publications.

Ress, G. J., & Snyder, J. (1994). *Forecasting and market analysis techniques: A practical approach.* Westport, CT: Quorum Books.

Rickman, T. A., & Cosenza, R. M. (2007). The changing digital dynamics of multichannel marketing: The feasibility of the weblog: Text mining approach for fast fashion trending. *Journal of Fashion Marketing and Management, 11*(4), 604–621.

Saffo, P. (2007, July-August). Six rules for effective forecasting. *Harvard Business Review.* Retrieved from http://hbr.org/2007/07/six-rules-for-effective-forecasting/ar/1

Sales forecasting. (n.d.). Reference for Business. *Encyclopedia of Business* (2nd ed.). Retrieved from http://www.referenceforbusiness.com/encyclopedia/Res-Sec/Sales- Forecasting.html

Sales Records. (2010). *Entrepreneur*. Retrieved from http://www.entrepreneur.com/encyclopedia/term/82582.html

Sproles, G. B., & Burns, L. D. (1994). *Changing appearances: Understanding dress in contemporary society*. New York: Fairchild Publications.

StatSoft. (n.d.). *Demand forecasting*. Retrieved from http://www.statsoft.com/textbook/demand-forecasting/

Stone, E. (2008). *The dynamics of fashion* (3rd ed.). New York: Fairchild.

Swanson, K. K., & Everett, J. C. (2000). *Promotion in the merchandising environment*. New York: Fairchild Publications.

Trenzza Design Studio. (n.d.). Color boards/Mood boards. Retrieved from http://www.trenzza.com/color-boards.html

Trenzza Design Studio. (n.d.). Trend boards. Retrieved from http://www.trenzza.com/trend-boards.html

INDEX

using quantitative and qualitative
techniques, 87–8
sales history, 87
scenario writing, 56
seamless knitting, 121
secondhand garments, 122
September 11, 2001, 5
shifting erogenous zones, 17
short-term forecasting, 49
Simmel, Georg, 12
simultaneous-adoption theory, 12
    see also mass-market theory; trickle-
        across theory
smart fabrics, 121
smart phones, 150
social networking, 110–11
social pressure, 3
social responsibility
    definitions, 119–20
sociocultural context, 49
soya bean fibers, 125
status float phenomenon, 13
    see also trickle-up theory
status symbol, 14
stock-keeping-unit (SKU), 88
style
    defining, 2
    as forecasting, 63–5
style-confident consumer, 97–8, 103
Stylesight, 76, 77
stylists, 72, 90
survey, 81
sustainability, 52, 119–20
sustainable competitive advantage, 82–3
sustainable design, 122
Sustainable Style Foundation (S.S.F.),
    136, 138
synthesis, 49

Target, 51, 98, 101–2
technological advances, 5
    see also technological inventions
technological inventions, 8
    see also technological advances
Textile Color Card Association of America
    (TCCA), 19, 73

see also Color Association of the United
    States (CAUS)
textiles
    as forecasting, 62
threadless.com, 107
time-series analysis, 85
Tobe Report, 76
Ton, Tommy, 87
trade shows, 48, 59, 78–9
trend, 2
    analysis, 46
    board, 145–6, 152
    book, 144–5
    defining, 1
    forecasting, 143
        companies, 60
    map, 144
        directional trends, 144
        embryonic trends, 144
        trial balloons, 144
    services, 63
    spotters, 56
    spotting, 56
Trent Westside, 103–4
trialability, 27
trial stage, 25, 109
Triangulation of data, 113
trickle-across theory, 12–13
    see also mass-market theory; simultaneous-
        adoption theory
trickle-down theory, 11–12
trickle-up theory, 13–14

Undesigned, 130–1
Ungaro, Emanuel, 9
Urban Outfitters, 65

Veblen, 11
Velvet Garden, 29–30
vendors, 88
Versace, Donatella, 23
virtual models, 108
visual and audio aides, 149
visual merchandisers, 72, 91
    as a promoter, 72
visual merchandising, 90